Primitive Psycho-Therapy and Quackery

By Robert Means Lawrence

They have observed but little, who have not remarked how much Imagination contributes to give success to the curative power of a medicine. VICESIMUS KNOX, D.D. Winter Evenings, I, p. 154.

The mind has the same command over the body, as the master over the slave. ARISTOTLE.

PREFACE

Certain historic modes of healing, including the use of medical amulets and charms, which have been regarded from early times as magical remedies, belong properly to the domain of Psychical Medicine. For the therapeutic virtues of medical amulets are not inherent in these objects, but are due to the influence exerted by them upon the imaginative faculties of the individuals who employ them. They afford powerful suggestions of healing. In this volume the writer has sought to emphasize the fact that the efficiency of many primitive therapeutic methods, and the success of charlatanry, are to be attributed to mental influence. The use of spells and incantations, the practice of laying-on of hands, the cult of relics, mesmerism, and metallo-therapy, have been important factors in the evolution of modern mental healing. The method of their operation, a mystery for ages, is revealed by the word suggestion. Thus may be traced some of the steps in the development of psycho-therapy. One ruling force, namely, the power of the imagination, has always been the potent therapeutic agent, whether in the word of command, in medical scripts, or in the methods of quackery. R. M. L.

177 BAY STATE ROAD, BOSTON, MASS. May 20, 1910.

CONTENTS

CHAPTER I

MEDICAL AMULETS

Among the various subjects which belong to the province of medical folk-lore, one of the most interesting relates to amulets and protective charms, which represent an important stage in the gradual development of Medicine as a science. And especially noteworthy among medical amulets are those inscribed with mystic sentences, words, or characters, for by their examination and study we may acquire some definite knowledge of the mental condition of the people who made use of them.

Satisfactorily to explain the derivation of the English word "amulet" has taxed the ingenuity of etymologists, and its origin is admittedly obscure. According to some authorities, the Latin amuletum was derived from amoliri, to avert or repel; but the greater weight of evidence points to the Arabic verb hamala, meaning "to carry." The definitions usually given embody both of these ideas; for amulets, in the ancient medical conception of the term, were any objects, ornamental or otherwise, worn on the bodies of men or animals, and believed to neutralize the ill effects of noxious drugs, incantations, witchcrafts, and all morbific agencies whatever.[4:1] To the Oriental mind amulets symbolize the bond between a protective power and dependent mundane creatures; they are prophylactics against the forces of evil, and may be properly characterized as objects superstitiously worn, whose alleged magical potency is derived from the faith and imagination of the wearer.[4:2]

The use of amulets has been attributed to religious sentimentality or religiosity. The latter word has been defined as "an excessive susceptibility to the religious sentiments, especially wonder, awe, and reverence, unaccompanied by any correspondent loyalty to divine law in daily life."[4:3]

Any one desirous of moralizing on the subject may find a theme presenting aspects both sad and comical. When, however, one reflects that amulets, in some one of their protean forms, have been invested with supernatural preventive and healing powers by the people of all lands and epochs, and that they have been worn not only by kings and princes, but by philosophers, prelates, and physicians of eminence as well, it is evident that the subject deserves more than a passing consideration.

It would be vain to seek the origin of their employment, which lies hidden behind the misty veil of remote antiquity. The eastern nations of old, as is well known, were much addicted to the use of amulets; and from Chaldea, Egypt, and Persia the practice was transmitted westward, and was thus extended throughout the civilized world. Among the great number of popular amulets in ancient times, many were fashioned out of metals, ivory, stone, and wood, to represent deities, animals, birds, and fishes; others were precious stones or cylinders inscribed with hieroglyphics; necklaces of shell or coral, crescent- or hand-shaped charms, and grotesque images. Their virtues were derived either from the material, from the shape, or from the magic rites performed at the time of their preparation. According to a popular belief, which prevailed throughout the East in the earlier centuries of the Christian era, all objects, whether inanimate stones and metals, or brutes and plants, possessed an indwelling spirit or soul, which was the cause of the efficiency of all amulets.[5:1] They were therefore akin to fetishes, in the present acceptation of the term; for a fetish, as defined in the classification of medicines and therapeutic agents in the collections of the National Museum at Washington, D. C., is a material object supposed to be the abode of a spirit, or representing a spirit, which may be induced or compelled to help the possessor.

According to Juvenal ("Satires," Book III, v, 1), Grecian athletes wore protective charms in the arena, to counterbalance the magical devices of their opponents. It is probable that the ethics of modern athletic contests would not countenance such expedients. But so implicit was the confidence of the Roman citizen in his amulet, that a failure to avert sickness or evil of any sort was not attributed to inherent lack of power in the charm itself, but rather to some mistake in the method of its preparation.[6:1]

In the time of the Emperor Hadrian (A. D. 76-138), and of his successors, the Antonines, the resources of occult science, known only to the initiated few, were believed to be sufficiently powerful, through the agency of spells and charms, to control the actions of evil spirits.[6:2] The early Christians readily adopted the pagan custom of wearing amulets as remedies against disease, and as bodily safeguards, in spite of the emphatic condemnation of the Church.

Origen (A. D. 186-253), a native of Alexandria, wrote that in his time it was customary for a person ailing from any cause to write certain characters on paper or metal, and fasten the amulet, thus improvised, upon the part of the body affected.[7:1] Passages from the books of the Gospel (literally "good spell") were especial favorites as such preservatives; they were usually inscribed on parchment, and were even placed upon horses.[7:2] Amulets were also employed to propitiate the goddess Fortune, and to thwart her evil designs. So insistent was the belief in the virtues of these objects, and to such a pitch of credulity did the popular mind attain, that special charms in great variety were devised against particular diseases, as well as against misfortunes and evil of whatever kind.[7:3]

Medieval astrology was a chief factor in promoting the use of amulets. Magic lent its aid to such an extent that, in certain lands, a chief part of Medicine consisted in the selection of suitable amulets against disease, and in their preparation.[7:4]

The almost universal dependence upon amulets, as prophylactics or healing agencies, originated through popular ignorance and fear.

With the advent of Christianity, many former superstitious beliefs were abandoned. Yet the process was very gradual.

The newest converts from paganism, while renouncing the forms which they had of necessity abjured, were disposed to attribute to Christian symbols some of the virtues which they had believed to inhere in heathen emblems and tokens.[8:1] The amulets and charms used by prehistoric man were silent appeals for protection against the powers of evil, the hostile forces which environed him.[8:2]

The doctrines of the Gnostics have been held by some writers to be responsible for the introduction of many amulets and charms in the early centuries of this era. Notwithstanding the fact (says Edward Berdoe in his "Origin of the Art of Healing") that the spirit of Christianity in its early day was strenuously opposed to all magical and superstitious practices, the nations which it subdued to the faith in Christ were so wedded to their former customs that they could not be entirely divorced from them. Thus, in the case of amulets, it was found necessary to substitute Christian words and tokens for their heathen counterparts.

Amulets and charms were much in vogue in ancient Egypt, and so great was the traditional reputation of the people of that country, as expert magicians, that throughout Europe in medieval times, strolling fortune-tellers and Gypsies were called Egyptians, and by this name they are still known in France. A written medical charm usually consisted of a piece of skin or parchment, upon which were inscribed a few words or mystic symbols. This was enclosed in a small bag or case, which was suspended from the wearer's neck.

The physician of the fifteenth century was wont to write his prescription in mysterious characters, and bind it upon the affected portion of the patient's body.[9:1]

In the rabbinical medicine, occult methods, involving astrology and the wearing of parchment amulets and charms, were more in evidence than the use of drugs; and among the inhabitants of ancient Babylon, traditional spells for driving out the demons of sickness were much employed.[9:2]

The forms of words embodied in charms and incantations were originally intended to be sung, and usually contained some rhyme, jingle, or alliterative verses.

The origin of these may be ascribed to the use of lullabies and cradle-songs, as a means of soothing infants, and lulling them to sleep. But formerly sick persons of all ages were comforted by these simple melodies. Dr. Joseph Frank Payne, in the "Fitz-Patrick Lectures," delivered at Oxford in 1904, remarked that many of the nursery rhymes of to-day are relics of literary forms which had formerly a deeper and sometimes a more formidable meaning.

For a goodly proportion of these magical therapeutic formulas had evidently a definite purpose, namely, the expulsion of the demons, who were believed to be the originators of disease.

Charm-magic, or the cure of disease through the instrumentality of written medical charms, may be properly classed as one method of utilizing the therapeutic force of suggestion. In ancient Assyria sacred inscriptions were placed upon the walls of the sick-room, and holy texts were displayed on either side of the threshold.

The Roman writer, Quintus Serenus Samonicus, author of "Carmen de Medicina," is said to have recommended as a cure for quartan ague, the placing of the fourth book of the Iliad under the patient's head.[10:1] Charm-magic has been regarded as a survival of animism, the theory which endows the phenomena of nature with personal life. It has also been defined as the explanation of all natural phenomena, not due to obvious material causes, by attributing them to spiritual agencies.

According to this view, the majority of superstitious fancies are of animistic origin. These include, not only many methods of primitive psycho-therapy, but also the belief in goblins, haunted houses, and the veneration of holy relics.

Magic writings have been and often are efficient psychic remedies for functional affections, in direct proportion to the user's faith in them. A certain sense of mystery seems essential. Given that, and plenty of confidence, and it matters not whether the inscriptions are biblical verses, unintelligible jargon, or even invocations of the Devil.

As an illustration of the attitude of the clergy towards the practice of heathen medical magic in Britain during the seventh century, we quote the words of an eminent French writer, St. Eligius, Bishop of Noyon (588-659), as recorded by the English ecclesiastical historian, Rev. Samuel Roffey Maitland (1792-1866), in his series of essays, entitled "The Dark Ages":--

Before all things I declare and testify to you that you shall observe none of the impious customs of the pagans, neither sorcerers, nor diviners, nor soothsayers, nor enchanters, nor must you presume for any cause, or for any sickness, to consult or inquire of them; for he who commits this sin loses unavoidably the grace of baptism. In like manner pay no attention to auguries, and sneezings; and when you are on a journey pay no attention to the singing of certain little birds. But whether you are setting out on a journey, or beginning any other work, cross yourself in the name of Christ, and say the Creed and the Lord's Prayer with faith and devotion, and then the enemy can do you no harm. . . . Let no Christian place lights at the temples, or the stones, or at fountains, or at trees . . . or at places where three ways meet, or presume to make vows. Let none presume to hang amulets on the neck of man or beast; even though they be made by the clergy, and called holy things, and contain the words of Scripture; for they are fraught, not with the remedy of Christ, but with the poison of the Devil. Let no one presume to make lustrations, nor to enchant herbs, nor to make flocks pass through a hollow tree, or an aperture in the earth; for by so doing he seems to consecrate them to the Devil.

Moreover, as often as any sickness occurs, do not seek enchanters, nor diviners, nor sorcerers, nor soothsayers, or make devilish amulets at fountains or trees, or cross-roads; but let him who is sick trust only to the mercy of God, and receive the sacrament of the body and blood of Christ with faith and devotion; and faithfully seek consecrated oil from the church, wherewith he may anoint his body in the name of Christ and according to the Apostle, the prayer of faith shall save the sick, and the Lord shall raise him up.

From very early times, says Lady Wilde, the pagan physicians of Ireland, who were famous as skilled practitioners, were prominent among the Druids. Although thoroughly conversant with the healing properties of herbs, they appreciated keenly the influence exerted upon the minds of their patients by charms, fairy cures, and incantations. Therefore their methods of treatment were of a medico-religious character, the psychic element being utilized in the form of various magic rites and ceremonies, which were important healing factors. The ancient Druidic charms are still in use among the Irish peasants, the titles of pagan deities being replaced, however, by the name of Christ and words of the Christian ritual. In this form they are regarded as magic talismans, when repeated over the sick, and the peasants have a strong faith in these mystic formulas, which have a powerful hold upon their imaginations, having been transmitted to them through many generations of a credulous ancestry.[13:1]

The peasants of Ireland do not wholly depend upon the skill of their fairy-women. On the contrary, every housekeeper has an intimate knowledge of the healing virtues of common herbs. The administration of these is always accompanied with a prayer. After domestic resources have been exhausted, especially if the ailment is believed to be of supernatural origin, recourse is had to the witch-doctress.

In a volume entitled "Beware of Pickpockets" (1605), being a warning against charlatans, occurs this passage:

Others, that they may colourably and cunningly hide their grosse ignorance, when they know not the cause of the disease, referre it unto charmes, witchcrafts, magnificall incantations and sorcerie. Vainely and with a brazen forehead, affirming that there is no way to help them but by characters, circles, figure-castings, exorcismes, conjurations and others impious and godlesse meanes. Others set to sale at a great price, certain amulets of gold and silver, stamped under an appropriate and selected constellation of the planets, with some magical characters, shamelessly boasting that they will cure all diseases and worke I know not what other wonders.

The employment of amulets involves the idea of protection against divers kinds of malicious spirits, including the demons of disease, ghosts, fairies, and evil-minded sprites, surly elves, fiends, trolls, pixies, bogies, kelpies, gnomes, goblins, witches, devils, imps, Jinn, et id omne genus. Amulets served as preventives against bodily ailments or injuries, misfortune and ill-luck generally.

Medieval practitioners, while utilizing material remedies to some extent, relied more on the resources of occult science, whether in the form of incantations or the revelations of astrology. The adept consulted the stars to determine the prognosis of a case of fever, for example. If he prescribed drugs only, his reputation suffered in the popular estimation. In order to be abreast of the times, the shrewd medieval physician needed to be well versed in star-craft, or at least to make a pretense thereto. It is probable that many patients would have despised a practitioner who looked only to his Herbal and store of drugs, and neglected Capricornus and Ursa Major.[14:1]

In "Chambers's Cyclopedia," published in 1728, an amulet is defined as a kind of medicament, hung about the neck, or other part of the body, to prevent or remove disease. And a charm is described as a magic power or spell, by which, with the assistance of the Devil, sorcerers and witches were supposed to do wondrous things, far surpassing the power of Nature. According to popular opinion, medicines were of some value as remedies, but to effect radical cures the use of magic spells was desirable.

John Atkins wrote, in "The Navy Surgeon, or a Practical System of Surgery" (1737), that the best method of employing medical amulets consisted in adapting them to the patients' imaginations. "Let the newness and surprise," wrote he, "exceed the invention, and keep up the humor by a long roll of cures and vouchers; by these and such means, many distempers, especially of women, who are ill all over, or know not what they ail, have been cured more by a fancy to the physician than by his prescription. Quacks again, according to their boldness and way of addressing, command success by striking the fancies of an audience."

Edward Berdoe, in the "Origin and Growth of the Healing Art," comments on the universality of amuletic symbols and talismans. They are peculiar to no age or region, and unite in one bond of superstitious brotherhood the savage and the philosopher, the Sumatran and the Egyptian, the Briton and the native of Borneo. When a medical written charm is wholly unintelligible, its curative virtue is thereby much enhanced. The Anglo-Saxon document known as the Vercelli manuscript by some means found its way to Lombardy. Its text being undecipherable, the precious pages of the manuscript were cut up, to serve as amulets.

Apropos of this subject, Charles M. Barrows, in "Facts and Fictions of Mental Healing," remarks that whatever acts upon a patient in such a way as to persuade him to yield himself to the therapeutic force constantly operative in Nature, is a means of healing. It may be an amulet, a cabalistic symbol, an incantation, a bread-pill, or even sudden fright. It may be a drug prescribed by a physician, imposition of hands, mesmeric passes, the touch of a relic, or visiting a sacred shrine.

Dr. Samuel McComb, in "Religion and Medicine,"[16:1] remarks that the efficacy of the amulets and charms of savages depends upon the fact that they are symbols of an inner mental state, the objects to which the desire or yearning could attach itself--in a word, they are auto-suggestions, done into wood and stone.

Professor Hugo Mussterberg has said that the less a patient knows about the nature of suggestion, the more benefit he is likely to experience therefrom; but that, on the contrary, a physician may obtain the better results, the more clearly he understands the working of this therapeutic agent.

It is also doubtless true that much good may result from the employment of suggestion by a charlatan, in the form of a written medical charm, both parties being alike profoundly ignorant of the healing influence involved.

In the Talmud, two kinds of medical amulets are specified, viz: the "approved" and the "disapproved." An approved amulet is one which has cured three persons, or which has been made by a man who has cured three persons by means of other amulets.[17:1] A belief in the healing power of amulets was very general among the Hebrews in the later periods of their history. No people in the whole world were more addicted to the use of medicinal spells, exorcisms, and various enchantments. The simpler amulets consisted of pieces of paper, with a few words written upon them, and their use was quite general. Only one of the approved kind was permitted to be worn abroad on the Sabbath.[17:2]

The Talmud therefore permits the use of superstitious modes of healing, the end sought justifying the means, and the power of mental influence being tacitly recognized. This principle is faithfully carried out to-day, says a writer in the "Journal of Biblical Literature,"[18:1] in all rural communities throughout the world. The Hebrew law-makers did not make a concession to a lower form of religion by endorsing magical remedies, but merely shared the contemporary belief in the demoniac origin of disease. The patient was regarded as being in a condition of enchantment or fascination,--under a spell, to use the popular phrase. To dissolve such a spell, recourse was had to amulets, written charms, or the spoken word of command.

FOOTNOTES:

[4:1] Carolus Christianus Krause, De Amuletis Medicis Cogitata Nonnulla, vol. iii, p. 4. Lipsia, 1758.

[4:2] Jo. Christianus Teutscherus, De Usu et Abusu Amuletorum. Lipsiensis, 1720.

[4:3] Century Dictionary.

[5:1] John William Draper, History of the Intellectual Development of Europe, vol. i, p. 392.

[6:1] Chambers's Journal, vol. xvi, p. 57; 1861.

[6:2] George F. Fort, Medical Economy during the Middle Ages, p. 78.

[7:1] The Reliquary, vol. vii, p. 162; 1893.

[7:2] James Townley, The Reasons of the Law of Moses, vol. ii, p. 944.

[7:3] Exercitationum Anatomico-Chirurgicarum Decades Du? De Amuletis. Lugd: Batavorum, 1708.

[7:4] Encyclopedie des Gens du Monde, art. "Amulette."

[8:1] The Catholic Encyclopedia.

[8:2] Elwood Worcester, D.D., Religion and Medicine.

[9:1] C. J. S. Thompson, The Mystery and Romance of Alchemy and Pharmacy, p. 124.

[9:2] Encyclopedia Biblica, art. "Medicine."

[10:1] William George Black, Folk-Medicine.

[13:1] Ancient Cures, Charms, and Usages of Ireland.

[14:1] George Roberts, The Social History of the People of the Southern Counties of England.

[16:1] New York, 1908, p. 94.

[17:1] Joseph Barclay, The Talmud.

[17:2] John Kitto, A Cyclopedia of Biblical Literature.

[18:1] Vol. xxiii, 1904.

CHAPTER II

TALISMANS

A talisman may be described as an emblematical object or image, accredited with magical powers, by whose means its possessor is enabled to enlist the aid of supernatural beings. Frequently it is a precious stone, sometimes a piece of metal or parchment, whereon is engraved a celestial symbol, such as the representation of a planet or zodiacal sign; or the picture of an animal or fabulous monster. Mystic words and occult phrases are oftentimes substituted, however, for such devices. It is essential that talismans should be prepared under suitable astrological conditions and planetary influences; otherwise they are of no value. Like amulets, they were formerly worn on the body, either as prophylactics or as healing agents. Tradition ascribes their invention to the Persian philosopher Zoroaster, but their use was probably coeval with the earliest civilizations: descriptions of cures wrought by medical talismans are to be found in the works of Serapion, a physician of the ancient sect of Empirics, who lived in Alexandria about 250 B. C.; and in those of Almansor (born 939), the minister of Hesham II, Sultan of Cordova.

Talismans were fashioned out of various metals, and their mystic virtues differed according to their forms and the symbols which they bore. Silver moon-shaped talismans, for example, were much in vogue as preservatives from fleshly ills; and they were also believed to insure travellers against mishaps.

In medieval times talismans and amulets were generally used as remedial agents. A mystical emblem, representing the inexpressible name of God, which was preserved at the Temple in Jerusalem, is found on many engraved gems. And two triangles, crossing each other, are said to have been the diagram of the Gnostics, with which many marvellous cures were performed.[20:1]

The pentacle, or wizard's foot, a mathematical figure, used in magical ceremonies, was considered to be a defence against demons. We read in Sir Walter Scott's "Marmion":

His shoes were marked with cross and spell: Upon his breast a pentacle.

This symbol, says C. J. S. Thompson, in "The Mystery and Romance of Alchemy and Pharmacy," consisted of a five-rayed star, and was often chalked upon the door-steps of houses, to scare away fiends. Thus it served the same purpose as the familiar horse-shoe, when the latter was placed with the prongs downward.

The belief in the pentacle's demon-repelling power has been attributed to the fact that it resolves itself into three triangles, and is thus a triple emblem of the Trinity. Paracelsus, according to the above-mentioned writer, ascribed a similar, although less marked virtue, to the hexagram.

The Tyrolese physician, Joseph Ennemoser, in his "History of Magic" (1844), observed that in his time a peculiar influence was attributed by mesmerists to certain metals and precious stones. And he expressed the belief that the popular faith in talismans, prevalent in the early ages, originated through similar ideas. The Buddhists credited the sapphire with magical power. Probably the magnetic polarities of jewels, rather than their brilliancy, constitute their chief potency as talismans. Yet the latter quality doubtless strongly influences the imagination.

Talismans were formerly divided into three classes, astronomical, magical, and mixed.

The first-named consisted usually of a magical figure, cut or engraved under certain superstitious observances of the configuration of the heavens.

It has been defined as the seal, figure, character, or image of a heavenly sign, constellation, or planet, engraved on a sympathetic stone, or on a metal corresponding to the star, in order to receive its influences.[22:1]

Magical talismans were inscribed with mysterious symbols, words of superstitious import, and the names of unknown angels; they were well adapted to inspire with awe the minds of the ignorant. The so-called mixed talismans bore various unintelligible devices and barbaric names. Some of the most ancient protective and healing charms were fashioned out of roots, twigs, and plants. Whatever its form, the talisman was believed to exert an extraordinary influence over the bearer, especially in warding off disease or injury.

In its widest sense, the word talisman is synonymous with amulet.

The Dutch historian, Johann Busch (1400-1477), told of his meeting a woman, the wife or daughter of a soldier, on some public festal occasion at Halle in Prussian Saxony. Observing that she wore a little bag suspended from her neck, he asked her what it contained. Thereupon the woman showed him a bit of parchment bearing divers mystic inscriptions, and the statement that Pope Leo guaranteed the bearer thereof against bodily injuries, fainting spells, and drowning. Then followed the words, Christus vincit; Christus regnat, together with the names of the twelve apostles, and those of the three Wise Men, Balthasar, Melchior, and Kaspar.[23:1]

This doubtless was a fair specimen of the inscribed amulets, worn by German peasants in the fifteenth century.

Even nowadays the names of the three magi are often to be seen, as talismanic symbols, upon the doors and walls of dwellings in certain Roman Catholic countries; a fact noted by the present writer, while sojourning in the Austrian Tyrol a few years ago.

FOOTNOTES:

[20:1] M. F. Blumler, A History of Amulets.

[22:1] The Century Dictionary.

[23:1] Johann Heinrich Zedler, Grosses Universal Lexicon, art. "Talismans." Leipzig und Halle, 1744.

CHAPTER III

PHYLACTERIES

They ware in their foreheads scrowles of parchment, wherein were written the tenne commaundements given by God to Moses, which they called philaterias. JOHN MARBECK, Book of Notes and Common-Places: 1581.

There were Phylacteries for the head, reaching from one ear to the other, and tied behind with a thong; and Phylacteries for the hand, fastened upon the left arme, above the elbow, on the inside, so that it might be near the heart. THOMAS GODWIN, Moses and Aaron: 1616.

Among the Greeks of the first century A. D. the word phylacterion (from +phylassein+, to guard, and equivalent to the Roman amuletum) signified a portable charm, which was believed to afford protection against disease and evil spirits. Such charms, in their simplest form, consisted of rolls of parchment or ribbon, inscribed with magical spells, and were hung around the wearer's neck, or attached to the hem of his garment. Among the Hebrews and early Christians similar protectives were used, although the latter substituted Gospel texts for the magic formulas. Some authorities have maintained that phylacteries were not strictly amulets, but it is certain that they were held in superstitious regard.[25:1] More elaborate phylacteries consisted of tiny leathern boxes, cubical in form, and containing four sections of the Mosaic Law, written on parchment and folded in the skin of a clean beast. These were carried either upon the head or left arm.[25:2]

The custom of wearing portions of the Gospels, suspended from the neck, was common in the East. Pope Gregory the Great (540-604) sent to Theodelinda, Queen of the Lombards, a box containing a copy of the Gospels, as a charm against the evil spirits which beset children.[25:3] The origin of this practice is found in Deuteronomy VI, 6-9: "And these words, which I command thee this day, shall be in thine heart: And thou shalt teach them diligently unto thy children, and shalt talk of them when thou sittest in thine house, and when thou walkest by the way, and when thou liest down, and when thou risest up. And thou shalt bind them for a sign upon thine hand, and they shall be as frontlets between thine eyes. And thou shalt write them upon the posts of thy house, and on thy gates."

In the rabbinical Targum, the Aramaic translation of the Bible, canto VIII, written about A. D. 500, occurs this passage: "The congregation of Israel hath said, I am chosen above all people, because I bind the Phylacteries on my left hand and on my head, and the scroll is fixed on the right side of my door, the third part of which is opposite my bed-room, that the evil spirits may not have power to hurt me."

Thus it would appear that the saying quoted by Grimm, "Christians place their faith in words, the Jews in precious stones, and the Pagans in herbs," is not wholly correct, for the Jews added to a trust in stones, a faith in the long, embroidered, text-inscribed phylactery.[26:1]

At the beginning of the Christian era, the belief was general among the Jews and pagans, that by means of magical formulas the evil influence of the Devil and demons could be successfully resisted. Therefore the Hebrew exorcists found easily a fertile soil for the cultivation of their supernatural art. This, says a writer in the "Jewish Encyclopedia," was the atmosphere in which Christianity arose, with the claim of healing all that were oppressed of the Devil. The name of Jesus became the power by which the host of Satan was to be overcome. But pharisaism diagnosed the disease of the age differently, and insisted that the observance of the Law was the best prophylactic against disease. The wearing of phylacteries indicates that they were regarded by the Jews as amulets. Belief in the power of the Law became the antidote against what may be termed "Satanophobia," a pessimistic and habitual dread of devils and demons.

The wearing of phylacteries is a fundamental principle of the Jewish religion. They are to be preserved with the greatest care. Indeed, the Rabbis assert that the single precept of the phylacteries is equal in value to all the commandments.[27:1] The Talmud says: "Whoever has the phylacteries bound to his head and arm, and the fringes thrown over his garments, and the Mezuza[27:2] fixed on his door-post, is safe from sin; for these are excellent memorials, and the angels secure him from sin; as it is written, 'The angel of the Lord encampeth round about them that fear him, and delivereth them.'"[27:3] Maimonides, the Jewish philosopher of the twelfth century, extolled the sacred influence of the phylacteries. For as long as one wears them on his head and arm, he is obliged to be meek and God-fearing, and must not suffer himself to be carried away by laughter or idle talk, nor indulge in evil thoughts, but must turn his attention to the words of truth and uprightness.

In order to emphasize their religious zeal, the Pharisees and scribes, in our Lord's time, were wont to "make broad their phylacteries."[27:4] Josephus, the historian of the first century, speaks of the wearing of phylacteries, as an established and recognized custom. According to the Cabala, they were significant of the wisdom and greatness of God, and their use distinguished the cultured and pious from the common people, who were ignorant of the Law.

Great care was taken in the preparation of phylacteries, and no Christian, apostate, or woman was allowed to write the inscriptions upon them. Even at the present time, there are Jews in Russia and Poland, who wear them during the whole day.[28:1]

It was customary to tie certain kinds of phylacteries into a knot. Reference to this ancient practice is found in certain Assyrian talismans, now in the British Museum. Following is a translation of one of them: "Hea says: 'Go, my son! take a woman's kerchief, bind it round thy right hand; loose it from the left hand. Knot it with seven knots; do so twice. Sprinkle it with bright wine; bind it round the head of the sick man. Bind it round his hands and feet, like manacles and fetters; sit down on his bed; sprinkle water over him. He shall hear the voice of Hea. Darkness shall protect him, and Marduk, eldest son of Heaven, shall find him a happy habitation.'"[28:2]

While the practice of wearing phylacteries may not have originated in a superstitious belief in their virtues as "appurtenances to make prayers more powerful," it would appear that they came to be regarded not only as protective charms, which is indicated by their name, but also as magical remedies, having occult healing properties.[29:1] Their power was supposed to inhere in the written words, enclosed in the small leathern case.

At the present day, verses from the Scriptures, the Koran, and other sacred writings are sometimes worn upon the person and are also placed upon horses or camels, by Arabs, Turks, Grecians, and Italians, with the avowed purpose of averting malignant glances.[29:2]

FOOTNOTES:

[25:1] Encyclopedia Britannica.

[25:2] Samuel Burder, Oriental Customs, vol. ii, p. 226.

[25:3] Smith and Cheetham, A Dictionary of Christian Antiquities.

[26:1] William George Black, Folk-Medicine, p. 165.

[27:1] Joseph Barclay, The Talmud.

[27:2] Scroll of parchment, inscribed with passages of Scripture.

[27:3] Psalm xxxiv, 7.

[27:4] James Hastings, D.D., A Dictionary of Christ and the Gospels, 1908, p. 360. Matthew, xxiii, 5.

[28:1] Philip Schaff, D.D., A Religious Encyclopedia.

[28:2] Biblical Things not generally known, 1879, pp. 177-8. Marduk, the Chaldean Hercules.

[29:1] James Hastings, A Dictionary of the Bible.

[29:2] Frederick Thomas Elworthy, The Evil Eye.

CHAPTER IV

THE POWER OF WORDS

In every word there is a magic influence, and each word is in itself the breath of the internal and moving spirit. JOSEPH ENNEMOSER: The History of Magic.

There is magic in words, surely, and many a treasure besides Ali Baba's is unlocked with a verbal key. HENRY VAN DYKE: Little Rivers.

For it was neither herbs, nor mollifying plaster that restored them to health, but thy word, O Lord, which healeth all things. WISDOM OF SOLOMON, XVI, 12.

The power of words in stimulating the imagination is well expressed in the following sentences:--

Words, when well chosen, have so great a force in them, that a description often gives us more lively ideas than the sight of the things themselves. The reader finds a scene drawn in stronger colors, and painted more to the life in his imagination, by the help of words, than by an actual survey of the scene which they describe. In this case the poet seems to get the better of nature. He takes indeed the landscape after her, but gives it more vigorous touches, heightens its beauty, and so enlivens the whole piece, that the images which flow from the objects themselves, appear weak or faint in comparison with those that come from the expressions.[30:1]

The medical science of the ancient Romans was largely theurgical, and was founded on a pretended influence over spiritual beings, whether gods or demons. Their system of therapeutics included prayers, invocations, and magical sentences. In speaking of verbal charms, Lord Bacon commented on the fact that amongst the heathen nations, either barbarous words, without meaning, were used, or "words of similitude," which were intended to feed the imagination. Also religious texts, which strengthen that faculty. Mystical expressions were favorites, as were also Hebrew sentences, as belonging to the holy tongue. No examples of magical formulas are found in the Bible, but Rabbinical literature contains a large number of them, the majority being designated as "heathen," and their use forbidden.[31:1]

A belief in the potency of written or spoken words, for the production of good or evil, has been characteristic of all historic epochs and nations. The exorcist of ancient Egypt relied on amulets and mysterious phrases for the cure of disease; and a metrical petition traced on a papyrus-leaf, or a formula of prayer opportunely repeated, "put to flight the serpents, who were the instruments of fate."[31:2]

The efficacy anciently attributed to verbal charms appears to have been partly due to a current opinion that names of persons and things were not of arbitrary invention, but were in some mysterious manner evolved from nature, and hence were possessed of a certain inherent force, which was potent either for good or evil.[32:1]

Our Lord, when on earth, went about healing the sick by the sole power of words. A notable instance of this is the case of the centurion of Capernaum, who deemed himself unworthy of the honor of having Christ enter his dwelling, in order to cure his servant, who lay sick of the palsy. "But speak the word only," he said, "and my servant shall be healed." And the Master replied: "Go thy way; and as thou hast believed, so be it done unto thee." And his servant was healed in the self-same hour. That evening, we are told, many that were possessed with devils were brought unto him; and he cast out the spirits with his word, and healed all that were sick.[32:2] The popularity of

Scriptural texts in primitive therapeutics is doubtless largely due to the many wonderful cures wrought by words, which are recorded in the Bible.

Usually, in the Gospels, the healing word is addressed to the patient, but occasionally to his master, or to one of his parents. Whenever the belief in the power of sacred words appears outside of Holy Writ, it is generally expressed in the guise of a superstitious formula. This belief is found, however, in the mystical tenets of the ancient Jewish sect, known as the Essenes. It is also clearly stated in the Zend Avesta, as follows: "One may heal with herbs, one may heal with the Law, one may heal with the Holy Word; amongst all remedies, this is the healing one, that heals with the Holy Word; this one it is that will best drive away sickness from the body of the faithful; for this one is the best healing of all remedies."[33:1]

The religious and devotional sentences, which are so commonly seen above the entrances of dwellings in Germany and other European lands, and the passages from the Koran similarly used among Moslems, are not necessarily evidence of the piety of the members of a household. For, as has been remarked, these sentences are often regarded merely as protective charms.[33:2]

According to an old Welsh custom, fighting-cocks were provided with prophylactic amulets before entering the arena. These amulets consisted of biblical verses, inscribed on slips of paper, which were bound around the cocks' legs. A favorite verse thus used was Ephesians, VI, 16: "Taking the shield of faith, wherewith ye shall be able to quench all the fiery darts of the wicked."[33:3] Some of the old English medical verse-spells are sufficiently quaint exponents of popular credulity.

The following, for example, was in vogue as a remedy for cramp in the leg:--

"The Devil is tying a knot in my leg, Mark, Luke and John, unloose it, I beg."[34:1]

Mr. W. G. Black, in his "Folk-Medicine" (p. 170), remarks that many of the magic writings used as charms were nothing else than invocations of the Devil; and cites the case of a young woman living in Chelsea, England, who reposed confidence in a sealed paper, mystically inscribed, as a prophylactic against toothache. Having consented, at the request of her priest, to examine the writing, this is what she found: "Good Devil, cure her, and take her for your pains." This illustrates the somewhat trite proverb, "Where ignorance is bliss, 'twere folly to be wise," and is a proof of the wisdom of the popular belief that the inscription of a healing formula should not be seen by the wearer, inasmuch as its mystic words are ordinarily invocations of spiritual Beings, and are not therefore adapted for comprehension by the human intellect!

The mere remembrance of some traditional event in the life of our Lord has been accounted of value in popular leech-craft, as in the following charm against ague, taken from a diary of the year 1751, and still used in Lincolnshire within recent times: "When Jesus came near Pilate, he trembled like a leaf, and the judge asked Him if He had the ague. He answered that He neither had the ague nor was He afraid; and whosoever bears these words in mind shall never fear the ague or anything else."[35:1]

Eusebius of Caesarea, in his Ecclesiastical History,[35:2] gives the text of two letters alleged to have formed a correspondence between our Lord and Abgar, King of Edessa. They were said to have been originally written in Aramaic or Syro-Chaldaic characters, and were discovered beneath a stone some eighty miles from Iconium, the modern Konieh, in Asia Minor, in the year 97, and afterwards lost. Regarded as authentic by some learned authorities, they were nevertheless rejected as apocryphal by a church council at Rome, during the pontificate of Gelasius I, in the year 494. According to Eusebius, King Abgar, who was afflicted with a grievous sickness, learning of the wonderful cures wrought by our Lord, wrote Him a letter begging Him to come to Edessa. And the Master, although not acceding to this request, wrote a reply to the king, promising to send one of His disciples to heal him. And in fulfilment of that promise, after His resurrection, Thomas the Apostle, by divine command, sent Thaddeus, one of the seventy disciples, to Abgar. Such is the popular tradition. Full particulars of the visit of Thaddeus, together with copies of the letters taken from a Book of Records preserved at Edessa, may be found in a work entitled, "Ancient Syriac Documents," edited by W. Cureton, D.D. Copies of these letters were used as charms by the early Christians, and for this purpose were placed upon their door-lintels; they were still to be seen within recent years in many a cottage of Shropshire and Devon, where they are valued as preservatives from fever.[36:1] In the opinion of not a few scholars they are ingenious literary forgeries; but strong evidence in favor of their authenticity is afforded by the discovery, announced by Professor Bohrmann to the arch 鎜 logical congress at Rome, April 30, 1900, of copies of the same letters, inscribed in Doric Greek, in the stone-work above the gateway of the Palace of the Kings at Ephesus. The translated text of the rediscovered letters is as follows:

From Abgar to Christ: I have heard of Thee and the cures wrought by Thee without herb or medicine, for it is reported that Thou restoreth sight to the blind and maketh the lame to walk, cleanseth the leper, raiseth the dead, chaseth out devils and unclean spirits, and healeth those that are tormented of diseases of a long continuance. Hearing all this of Thee, I was fully persuaded that Thou art the very God come down from heaven to do such miracles, or that Thou art the son of God and performeth them. Wherefor I have sent Thee a few lines entreating Thee to come hither and cure my diseases. Hearing that the Jews murmur against Thee and continue to do Thee mischief, I invite Thee to my city, which is but a little one, but is beautiful and sufficient to entertain us both.

Christ's reply to Abgar: Blessed art thou for believing me when thou hast not seen, for it is written of me that they that have seen me shall not believe, and that they that have not seen me shall believe and be saved. But concerning the matter thou hast written about, this is to acquaint thee that all things for which I was sent hither must be fulfilled and that I shall be taken up and returned to Him that sent me. But after my ascension I will send one of my disciples that shall cure thee of thy distemper and give life to all them that are with thee.[37:1]

John Gaule, in the "Magastromancer,"[37:2] declares that sacred words derive their force from occult divine powers, which are conveyed by means of such words, "as it were through conduit-pipes, to those who have faith in them."

Among the Hindus, the mantra is properly a divinely inspired Vedic text; but quite generally at the present day it has degenerated into a mere spell for warding off evil; the original religious or moral precept being accounted of little force, when compared with the alleged magical potency of its component words.[37:3]

The exorcism of morbiferous demons was the chief principle of primitive therapeutics, and as a means to this end, the written or spoken word has always been thought to exert a very great influence. Possibly indeed in remote antiquity the art of writing was first applied in inscribing mystic words or phrases on parchment or other material, for use as spells.[38:1]

In treating the sick, the Apache medicine-man mumbles incoherent phrases, a method adopted quite generally by his professional brethren in many Indian tribes. He claims for such gibberish a mysterious faculty of healing disease. Much of its effectiveness, however, has been attributed to the monotonous intonation with which the words are uttered, and which tends to promote sleep just as a lullaby soothes an ailing child.[38:2]

It is noteworthy, however, that meaningless words have always been the favorite components of verbal charms, whose power, in the opinion of medieval conjurers, was in direct ratio to their obscurity;[38:3] and this fact is well shown in the incantations used by savages.

According to the late Dr. D. G. Brinton, the principle involved is, either that the gods are supposed to comprehend what men fail to understand; or else that the verbal charm represents "the god expressing himself through human organs, but in a speech unknown to human ears."[39:1] Reginald Scott expressed a popular modern idea of the force of certain words and characters, when he said that they were able of themselves to cure diseases, pull down, save, destroy and enchant, "without the party's assistance."[39:2]

The term incantation signifies a most potent method of magical healing; namely, "that resting on a belief in the mysterious power of words solemnly conceived and passionately uttered."[39:3]

In the belief of the Australian aborigines, "no demon, however malevolent, can resist the power of the right word."[39:4] Ignorant people are usually impressed by obscure phrases, the more so, if these are well sprinkled with polysyllables. Cicero, in his treatise on Divination (LXIV) criticizes the lack of perspicuity in the style of certain writers, and supposes the case of a physician who should prescribe a snail as an article of diet, and whose prescription should read, "an earth-born, grass-walking, house-carrying, unsanguineous animal." Equally efficacious might be the modern definition of the same creature as a "terrestrial, air-breathing, gastropodous mollusk." The degree of efficiency of such prescriptions is naturally in inverse proportion to the patient's mental culture. An average Southern negro, for example, affected with indigestion, might derive some therapeutic advantage from snail diet, but would be more likely to be benefited by the mental stimulus afforded by the verbose formula.

The Irish physicians of old had a keen appreciation of the healing influences of incantations upon the minds of their patients, and the latter had moreover a strong faith in the ancient Druidic charms and invocations. It is probable that in very early times, invocations were made in the names of favorite pagan deities. After the introduction of Christianity by Saint Patrick, the name of the Trinity and the words of the Christian ritual were substituted. Such invocations, when repeated in the presence of sick persons, are regarded by the Irish peasants of to-day as powerful talismans, effective through their magic healing power. So great is the faith of these simple people in the ancient hereditary cures, that they prefer to seek medical aid from the wise woman of the village, rather than from a skilled practitioner.[40:1]

The influence of the mind upon the physical organism, through the imagination, is well shown by the seemingly marvellous cures sometimes wrought by medical charms. But the efficacy of magical medicine has been usually proportionate to the degree of ignorance prevalent during any particular epoch. Yet some of the most famous physicians of antiquity had faith in superstitious remedies. The medical literature of the last century before Christ, and from that period until late in the Middle Ages, was an actual treasury of conjuration and other mummeries. Even the great Galen, who was regarded as an oracle, openly avowed his belief in the merits of magic cures.[41:1]

Galen wrote that many physicians of his time were of the opinion that medicines lost much of their efficacy, unless prescribed by their Babylonian or Egyptian names. They fully appreciated mental influence as a factor in therapeutics. Hence, instead of regular prescriptions, they sometimes wrote mystic formulas, which their patients either carried as charms, or rolled into pellets, which were then swallowed.[41:2]

In a "Book of Counsels to Young Practitioners" (1300) are to be found some interesting items regarding contemporary manners. Fledgling doctors are therein advised to make use of long and unintelligible words, and never to visit a patient without doing something new, lest the latter should say, "He can do nothing without his book." In brief, a reputation for infallibility must be maintained.

It is not surprising that curative spells were popular in the dark ages. A modern-writer[42:1] has been quoted as saying that these were to be used, not because they could effect direct physical changes, but because they brought the patient into a better frame of mind. We know that nervous affections were very prevalent in those times among the ignorant masses of the people, and verbal charms were doubtless of value in furnishing therapeutic mental impulses. The Germanic sooth-saying physicians maintained that every bodily ailment could be cured by the use of magical spells and enchanted herbs. The medieval charlatan oculists inherited ancient medical formulas, by means of which they professed to treat with success ophthalmic disorders. Their methods included the recitation of ritualistic words, accompanied with suitable gestures, and passes over the affected eyes.[42:2]

In Cotta's "Short Discoverie of the Unobserved Dangers of several sorts of Ignorant and Unconsiderate Practisers of Physicke in England" (1612) occur the following passages, quoted also by Brand, in "Popular Antiquities of Great Britain."[42:3]

If there be any good or use unto the health by spels, they have that prerogative by accident, and by the power and vertue of fancie. If fancie then be the foundation whereupon buildeth the good of spels, spels must needs be as fancies are, uncertaine and vaine. So must also, by consequent, be their use and helpe, and no lesse all they that trust unto them. . . . How can religion or reason suffer men that are not void of both, to give such impious credit unto an insignificant and senseless mumbling of idle words contrary to reason, without president of any truly wise or learned, and justly suspected of all sensible men?

In the early part of the seventeenth century, many diseases were regarded in the light of magic seizures. Therefore they were not amenable to treatment by materia medica. More could be accomplished through the patient's faith and imagination.

"Physicians," wrote the German scholar, Valentine Schindler, "do not discover and learn everything that they ought to know, in the universities; they have often to go to old wives, gypsies, masters of the Black Art, old peasant-folk, and learn from them. For these people have more knowledge of such things, than all the colleges and universities."[43:1]

The influence of technical language on the uneducated patient is exemplified in the effect produced on his mind by the mention of Latin names. The writer was impressed with this fact while engaged in dispensary practice some years ago. Such a patient, affected with mumps, for example, appears to experience a certain satisfaction, and is apt to be somewhat puffed up mentally as well as physically, when he learns that his ailment is Cynanche Parotid; and he expects a prescription commensurate with its importance.

The effective force of a verbal charm is increased by the rhythmic flow of its words; the solemn recitation or murmuring of mystic phrases. "Hence," said Jacob Grimm, "all that is strong in the speech wielded by priest, physician, or magician is allied to the forms of poetry."[44:1] In many a myth and fairy-tale, a cabalistic metrical verse pronounced by the hero causes wonderful results.[44:2]

As already intimated, the manner of reciting prayers, charms, and formulas was anciently deemed to be of more moment than the meaning of their constituent words. In Assyria, for example, healing-spells were repeated in a "low, gurgling monotone"; and in Egypt the magical force of incantations was largely due, in the popular mind, to their frequent repetition in a pleasing tone of voice.[44:3] The temper of mind which prompts words of good cheer, is in itself a healing charm of no mean value. For we read in the Book of Proverbs: "A merry heart doeth good like a medicine, but a broken spirit drieth the bones."[44:4]

In this progressive age, when men of science are seeking remedies against the so-called "dust nuisance," which at times renders walking in our streets a penance, it may not be amiss to call to mind an ancient spell for the removal of particles of dust or cinders from the eyes. This consisted in chanting the ninety-first psalm thrice over water, which was then used as a lotion for the eye.[45:1]

Popular faith in spells as therapeutic agents, an inheritance from Chaldea and Egypt, was still strong even at the dawn of modern times; and the force of medical charms was supplemented by various magic rites and by the ceremonial preparation of medicines.[45:2] The use of curative spells and characts comes within the province of white magic, which is harmless; so called to distinguish it from black magic, or the black art, which involves a compact with the Evil One. In rude ages the practice of the former as a means of healing, may be said to have found its justification in its philanthropic purpose.

According to Mungo Park, the natives of all portions of the Dark Continent are accustomed to wear written charms, called saphies, grigris, or fetiches, whose chief use is the warding-off or cure of disease. Although not themselves followers of Mohammed, the savages have entire confidence in these charms, which are supplied by Moslem priests; but their confidence is based upon the supposed magic of the writing, irrespective of its religious meaning.[46:1] The failure of a charm to perform a cure is attributed to the ingratitude and fickleness of the spirits.[46:2] In Algeria it is not an uncommon experience of physicians who have prescribed for native patients, to meet such an one some days after, with the prescription either suspended from his neck, or carefully hidden in his garments.[46:3] Evidently the sole idea of such a patient, in applying for advice, was to obtain a written formula to serve as an amulet. The Moslems of Arabia and Persia have a custom of applying to any stranger, preferably a European, for their protective written charms, which are the more highly esteemed if totally unintelligible to themselves. Such a practice, however, is not sanctioned by orthodox followers of the Prophet, who is said to have justified the use of healing-spells only upon condition that the inscribed words should be none other than the names of God, and of the good angels and jinn.[46:4]

The Hon. John Abercromby, in the second volume of his work entitled "Pre- and Proto-historic Finns,"[46:5] gives a vast number of the magic songs, or charms, of Finland, among which are to be found a collection of formulas, under the caption, "words of healing power," which were recited for the cure of physical ailments of every description. For the purpose of comparison the author has also grouped together many specimens of spells and incantations in vogue among the neighboring peoples, as the Swedes, Slavs, and Lithuanians. He is of the opinion that most of the magical Finnish songs were composed since the twelfth century, and in the transition period, before Christianity had fully taken the place of paganism. During this period the recitation of metrical charms was no longer restricted to the skilled magician, but became popular in every Finnish household. Hence apparently the gradual evolution of a mass of incantations for use in every conceivable exigency or emergency of life. A chief feature of many of these medical charms consists in vituperation and personal abuse of the particular spirit of sickness addressed.

The peasants of Greece have long been addicted to the use of charms for the cure of various ailments. Following is the translation of a spell against colic which is in vogue amongst them: "Good is the householder, wicked is the housewife; she cooks beans, she prepares oil, vine-cuttings for a bed, stones for a pillow; flee pain, flee colic; Christ drive thee hence with his silver sword and his golden hand." According to Dr. N. G. Polites, this charm originated in a tradition that Christ when on earth begged a night's lodging at a house, the mistress whereof was ill-tempered and unkind to the poor, while her husband was hospitably disposed toward needy wayfarers. The husband being absent, his wife bade Christ take shelter in the barn, and later provided him with some beans for supper, while she and the master of the house fared more sumptuously. In the night the woman had a severe colic, which the usual domestic remedies failed to relieve; and her husband appealed to the poor wayfarer, who at once exorcised the demon of colic.[48:1]

Written charms were usually worn exposed to view, in order that evil spirits might see them and read their inscriptions. In course of time they developed into ornaments. Wealthy Hebrews were wont to carry amulets made of gold, silver, bronze, and precious stones; while their poorer brethren were contented with modest bits of parchment, woolen cloth, or lace.[48:2] In eastern countries a common variety of charm consists of a small piece of paper or skin, duly inscribed. Manifold are the virtues ascribed to such a charm! It may enable the bearer to find hidden treasure, to win the favor of a man or woman, or to recover a runaway wife.[48:3]

A written medical prescription of to-day, after having been filled and copied by a druggist, is usually considered to have fulfilled its mission, but the annals of popular medicine afford ample evidence of the narrowness of such a view! The practice of swallowing the paper whereon a recipe is written, as a veritable charm-formula, is of great antiquity, and is still in vogue in many lands. The idea involved in this singular custom is of course a superstitious regard for writing as a magical curative.

In endeavoring to trace the origins of this and other analogous usages, one must study the records of the most ancient civilizations. Among various African tribes, written spells, called saphies, are commonly used as medicines by the native wizards, who write a prayer on a piece of wood, wash it off with water, and cause the patient to drink the solution.[49:1] Mungo Park, while in West Africa, was once asked by his landlord, a Bambarra native, to prepare such a charm, the latter proffering his writing-board for the purpose. The traveller complied, and the negro, while repeating a prayer, washed the writing off with water, drank the mixture, and then licked the board dry, in his anxiety to derive the greatest possible benefit from the writing.[49:2]

The eating of the paper on which a prescription has been written is still a common expedient for the cure of disease in Tibet, where the Lamas use written spells, known as "edible letters."[50:1] The paper containing cabalistic words and symbols, taken internally, constitutes the remedy, and through its influence on the imagination is probably more beneficial to the patient than are most of the so-called "bitters" and patent medicines of the present day.

So likewise, when a Chinese physician cannot procure the drugs which he desires in a particular case, he writes the names of these drugs on a piece of paper, which the patient is expected to eat;[50:2] and this mode of treatment is considered quite as satisfactory as the swallowing of the medicine itself. Sometimes a charm is burned over a cup of water, and the ashes stirred in, and drunk by the patient, while in other cases it is pasted upon the part of the body affected.[50:3]

In eastern countries generally, remedial qualities are ascribed to water drunk out of a cup or bowl, whose inner surface is inscribed with religious or mystical verses; and specimens of such drinking-vessels have been unearthed in Babylonia within recent years. The magic medicine-bowls, still used in the Orient, usually bear inscriptions from the Koran.[50:4] In Flora Annie Steel's tale of the Indian Mutiny of 1857, "On the Face of the Waters" (p. 293), we read of a native who was treated for a cut over the eye by being dosed with paper pills inscribed with the name of Providence.

Dr. John Brown of Edinburgh (1810-1882) reported the case of a laboring man affected with colic, for whom he prescribed some medicine, directing him to "take it and return in a fortnight," assuring him that he would soon be quite well. At the appointed time the man returned, entirely relieved and jubilant. The doctor was gratified at the manifest improvement in his patient's condition, and asked to see the prescription which he had given him; whereupon the man explained that he had "taken" it, as he had understood the directions, by swallowing the paper.

In Egypt, at the present time, faith in the power of written charms is generally prevalent, and forms one of the most characteristic beliefs of the people of that country.

E. W. Lane, in "Modern Egyptians," says that the composition of these characts is founded chiefly upon magic, and devolves usually upon the village schoolmasters. They consist of verses from the Koran, and "names of God, together with those of angels, genii, prophets, or eminent saints, intermixed with combinations of minerals, and with diagrams, all of which are supposed to have great secret virtues."

One of the most popular Egyptian methods of charming away disease is similar to a practice already mentioned as in use among less civilized peoples.

The sacred texts are inscribed on the inner surfaces of earthenware bowls, in which water is stirred until the writing is washed off. Then the infusion is drunk by the patient, and without doubt the subsequent benefit is exactly commensurate with the strength of his faith in the remedy.

FOOTNOTES:

[30:1] Joseph Addison, On the pleasures of the Imagination.

[31:1] The Jewish Encyclopedia.

[31:2] G. Maspero, The Dawn of Civilization, p. 214.

[32:1] Larousse, Dictionnaire, art. "Charme."

[32:2] Matthew, viii, 8, 13, 16.

[33:1] Encyclopedia Biblica, art. "Medicine," T. K. Cheyne and J. Sutherland Black.

[33:2] Elworthy, The Evil Eye, p. 400.

[33:3] Elias Owen, Welsh Folklore, p. 245.

[34:1] Robley Dunglison, Medical Dictionary, p. 202.

[35:1] Notes and Queries, 4th series, vol. vii, p. 443. For other versions of this charm see W. G. Black, Folk-Medicine, p. 82; Pettigrew, Medical Superstitions, p. 57.

[35:2] Book i, ch. 13.

[36:1] Notes and Queries, 5th Series, vol. i, pp. 325, 375.

[37:1] Boston Transcript, May 2, 1900.

[37:2] London, 1652, p. 231.

[37:3] Monier-Williams, Religious Thought in India, p. 197.

[38:1] C. W. King, Early Christian Numismatics, p. 179.

[38:2] Annual Report of the Bureau of Ethnology, Washington, D. C., 1887-8, p. 453.

[38:3] R. M. Lawrence, The Magic of the Horse-Shoe, p. 300.

[39:1] Religions of Primitive Peoples, p. 93.

[39:2] A Discourse concerning the Nature and Substance of Devils and Spirits,

p. 70; 1665.

[39:3] M'Clintock and Strong, Cyclopedia, art. "Incantation."

[39:4] D. G. Brinton, Religions of Primitive Peoples, p. 91.

[40:1] Lady Wilde, Ancient Charms, Cures, and Usages of Ireland.

[41:1] Dr. Hugo Magnus, Superstition in Medicine.

[41:2] Otto A. Wall, M.D., The Prescription.

[42:1] H. D. Traill, Social England, vol. ii, p. 112.

[42:2] George F. Fort, Medical Economy of the Middle Ages, p. 195.

[42:3] Vol. iii, p. 322.

[43:1] Johannes Janssen, History of the German People at the Close of the Middle Ages.

[44:1] Teutonic Mythology, vol. iii, p. 1223.

[44:2] Andrew Lang, Myth, Ritual, and Religion, vol. i, p. 101.

[44:3] T. Witton Davies, Magic, Divination, and Demonology, p. 127.

[44:4] Proverbs, xvii, v. 22.

[45:1] London Spectator.

[45:2] M'Clintock and Strong, art. "Incantation."

[46:1] Travels, p. 56.

[46:2] Mary H. Kingsley, Travels in West Africa, p. 304.

[46:3] Musine, t. ix, p. 132; 1898.

[46:4] Thomas Patrick Hughes, A Dictionary of Islam, art. "Da'wah."

[46:5] London, 1898.

[48:1] Academy, vol. xxxi, p. 291; 1887.

[48:2] Michael L. Rodkinson, History of Amulets, Charms, and Talismans.

[48:3] George H. Bratley, The Power of Gems and Charms.

[49:1] Sir John Lubbock, The Origin of Civilization.

[49:2] Travels, vol. i, p. 357.

[50:1] L. Austin Waddell, The Buddhism of Tibet, p. 401.

[50:2] Edward Berdoe, Origin and Growth of the Healing Art, p. 133.

[50:3] Hampton C. Du Bose, The Dragon, Image and Demon, p. 407.

[50:4] Austen H. Layard, Nineveh and Babylon, p. 417.

CHAPTER V

THE CURATIVE INFLUENCE OF THE IMAGINATION

At the present day the remarkable benefit which often results from hygienic and mental influences combined is well shown in the so-called Kneipp cure, originated by Sebastian Kneipp, formerly parish priest of Wishofen in Bavaria. Briefly, its chief principles are simple diet, the application of water by means of wet sheets, douches, hose, or watering-pots; the covering of the wet body with dry underwear; and stimulation of the imagination, together with physical invigoration, by long walks afield barefoot, or with sandals; and lastly, music and mental diversions. In a word, a modernized Esculapian treatment.

The remedial virtue of verbal charms and incantations is derived from the human imagination, and upon this principle is founded the art of mental therapeutics. The idea of a cure being formed in the mind reacts favorably on the bodily functions, and thus are to be explained the successful results oftentimes effected under the methods known as Christian Science, Mind Cure, and Faith Cure.[53:1] Mrs. Mary Baker Eddy, the founder of the first-named system, avows that Christian Healing places no faith in hygiene or medicines, but reposes all trust in mind, divinely directed.[54:1] She declares that the subconscious mind of an individual is the only agent which can produce an effect upon his body.[54:2] There is undoubtedly much that is good in the doctrines of the Christian Scientists; but a fatal mistake therein is their contempt for skilled medical advice in sickness. God has placed within our reach certain remedies for the relief or cure of many bodily ailments; and whoever fails to provide such remedies for those dependent upon him, when the latter are seriously ill, is thereby wickedly negligent. Mental influence is oftentimes extremely valuable, but it cannot always be an efficient substitute for opium or quinine, when prescribed by a competent practitioner. We read in Ecclesiasticus, XXXVIII, 4, 10, 12: "The Lord hath created medicines out of the earth, and he that is wise will not abhor them. . . . My son, in thy sickness be not negligent, but pray unto the Lord, and He will make thee whole. . . . Then give place to the physician, for the Lord hath created him. Let him not go from thee, for thou hast need of him."

In treatises on suggestive therapeutics stress is laid upon the exaltation of the imaginative faculty induced by hypnotism; and it is well known that during induced sleep this faculty accepts as real impressions which would not pass muster if inspected by the critical eye of the waking intelligence. The whole secret of cures alleged to have been wrought by animal magnetism or mesmerism, may be explained by mental influence; and so likewise those affected by metallic tractors, anodyne necklaces, and a host of other devices. We have indeed an intelligible explanation of the rationale of many therapeutic methods in vogue at different periods of the world's history.

But, to recur to Christian Science, or Eddyism, it is certain that the alleged cures of organic affections, by the methods of that system, are not genuine. The many cases benefited by those methods have been and are such as are amenable to mental healing, of whatever kind. A writer in the "American Medical Quarterly," January, 1900, avers that Eddyism is an intellectual distemper, of a contagious character; that it is epidemic in this country, and that, in its causation, its rise and spread, it presents a close analogy to the great epidemics of history.

The ancient magicians, in their various methods of treating the sick, strove ever after sensational means of healing, and their example has been closely followed by the quacks of every succeeding age. They failed to appreciate that a tablet of powdered biscuit, discreetly administered, may be as beneficial therapeutically as any relic of a holy saint, because the healing force in either case is wholly mental, and resides in the patient. The exceptional notoriety achieved by Paracelsus was largely due to his shrewdness in pandering to the love of the marvellous, while utilizing also bona-fide materia medica.

Indeed, however strong may have been the belief in magical agencies as healing factors, the most eminent early practitioners were ever ready to avail themselves of material remedies. For they maintained that the actions of the physician should not be hampered by metaphysical considerations.[56:1] Not only did the magicians employ precious stones and metals as remedies, on account of their intrinsic value and the popular belief in their virtues, but they also prescribed the most loathsome and repulsive substances. The early pharmacopoeias and the works of noted charlatans, together with the annals of folk-medicine, afford ample evidence of this fact.

Apropos of this subject, we quote from a lecture given by Dr. Richard Cabot at the Harvard Medical School, February 13, 1909:--

In one of our great hospitals here it has been the custom for a long time to use for treatment by suggestion a tuning-fork which is known at that hospital as a magnet. It is not a magnet; it is merely an ordinary, plain, rather large tuning-fork. But people have, as you know, a very curious superstition about the action of magnets, and believing this tuning-fork to be a magnet, they attribute occult and wonderful powers to it. When placed upon a supposedly paralyzed limb or on the throat of a person who thinks he cannot speak, it has wonderful powers just because it is supposed to be a magnet, when in fact it is a tuning-fork. I remonstrated once with the gentleman who uses this tuning-fork because, so far as I could see, it was a lie, like all other forms of quackery; but he said, "Why, no, it does a great deal of good; it cures the patients." I replied that I had no doubt of that. So does skunk oil and Omega oil; so does the magic handkerchief which Francis Truth has touched; so does the magic ring, the electric belt, and the porous plaster. They all cure, but they all deceive people, in so far as one supposes that something is going on which is not revealed, something like imaginary electricity in the ring, something like the supposed medical activity in the porous plaster. In another great hospital in this city electricity is used in the same way. Electricity has medical action of course, in some cases, but it is used also in a great number of cases where it is not supposed to have any medical action because it has so strong a psychical action. When one sees a brass instrument that looks like a trident approaching one's body, and feels long crackling sparks shoot out of its prongs against one's body, it naturally makes a very strong impression upon one's mind.

How psychological methods may be employed in everyday life was the subject of an address by Professor Hugo Musterberg, of Harvard University, before the Commercial Club of Chicago, December 13, 1908. The success of these methods in the field of medicine is attested by the constantly increasing number of cures of nervous and other affections. "There is no magic fluid," he said, "no mysterious power afloat; it is just a state of mind. Every one can suggest something to every one else. It is the idea that is strong enough to overcome the idea in another mind that produces the effects wondered at. Hypnotism is only reinforced suggestion. It is a tool which no physician should be without."

Psychological knowledge, according to the same authority,[58:1] is gradually leaking into the world of medicine. The power of suggestion, with its varied methods, is slowly becoming a most important therapeutic agent in the hands of reputable practitioners. The time has arrived when medical students, about to enter upon professional life, should be equipped with a knowledge of scientific psychology. Physicians do not now deserve sympathy, if they are dumfounded when quacks and pretenders are successful where their own attempts at curing have failed. It is evident, however, that reform in this field is at hand, and it may be admitted that even those knights-errant have helped, after many centuries, to direct the public interest to the paramount importance of psychology in medicine.

We may cite the invocations of the Egyptian priests to obtain a cure from each god for those submitted to his influence; the magic formulas, which taught the use of herbs against disease; the medicine of Esculapius's descendants, the Asclepiads, an order of Greek physicians, who practised medicine under the reputed inspiration of that deity, and were bound by oath not to reveal the secrets of their art. Is it necessary to speak of the king's touch, of the miraculous cures at the tomb of the French ascetic priest, Francis Paris (1690-1727), and especially of Lourdes, and other noted pilgrimage resorts? Many professional healers may be mentioned, "of whom some were honest and believed themselves to be endowed with supernatural powers like certain magnetisers, and who used suggestion without knowing it, as for example the Irishman Greatrakes (1628-1700), the German priest Gassner (1727-1779), and many others whose fame does not extend beyond the region where they exercised their mysterious power."[59:1]

In the same category, as regards their modus operandi, may be classed medical charms and healing-spells. These serve also to inspire hope, or the expectation of cure, in the patient's mind, and thus act as tonics; they may also be useful as a means of diverting the mind of a hypochondriac, and changing the current of his thoughts, in which sense they may be classed as mental alteratives.

Allusion has been made to the magical spells, of ancient repute among the Hindus, which are known as mantras. They are available for sending an evil spirit into a man, and for driving it out; for inspiring love or hatred; and for causing disease or curing it. The Hindus do not repose confidence in a physician, unless he knows, or assumes to know, the proper mantra for the cure of any ailment. And this is the reason why European practitioners, who are not addicted to the use of spells, do not find favor among them. The medical men who pretend to be versed in occult lore, whether charlatans or magicians, are ready to furnish suitable mantras at short notice, whether for healing, for the recovery of stolen property, or for any other conceivable purpose.[60:1] The ethics of quackery are probably on the same plane everywhere; and not only are the spells forthcoming, if sufficient compensation be assured, but they are also more or less effective, through the power of suggestion, as therapeutic agents.

In nervous affections, where the imagination is especially active, amulets and healing-spells exert their maximum effect.[60:2] No one, however cultured or learned, is wholly unsusceptible to the physical influence of this faculty of the mind; and it has been well said that everybody would probably be benefited by the occasional administration of a bread-pill at the hand of a trusted medical adviser.[61:1] But faith on the patient's part is essential. Pettigrew, in his work on "Medical Superstitions," illustrates this by an example whose pertinence is not lessened by a dash of humor. A physician, who numbered among his patients his own father and his wife's mother, was asked why his treatment in the former case had been more successful than in the latter. His reply was that his mother-in-law had not as much confidence in him as his father had, and therefore had failed to receive as much benefit. Similarly, if a verbal charm is to cure a physical ailment, the patient must first form a mental conception of the cure, and believe in the charm's efficacy. But faith in healing-spells of human devising is sometimes cruelly misplaced, as is shown in the following anecdote, taken from the writings of Godescalc de Rozemonde, a Belgian theologian. A woman, suffering from a painful affection of the eyes, applied to a student for a magical writing to charm away the trouble, and promised him a new coat as a recompense. The student, nothing loath, wrote a sentence on a piece of paper, which he rolled in some rags and gave to the woman, telling her to carry the charm always about her, and on no account to read the writing. The woman gladly complied, was cured of her eye-trouble, and loaned the charm to another woman, similarly affected, who also soon experienced relief. Thereupon a natural curiosity prompted them to examine the mystic spell, and this is what they read: "May the Devil pluck out thine eyes, and replace them with mud!"

In "Folk-Lore," for September, 1900, there is an interesting article, giving an account of popular beliefs current in a remote village of Wiltshire, England, where medicines are usually regarded as charms. A man who had pleurisy was told by his doctor to apply a plaster to his chest. On the doctor's next visit, he was informed that his patient was much better and that the plaster had given great relief. Failing, however, on examination of the man's chest, to find any sign of counter-irritation of the skin, he was somewhat puzzled; but he soon learned from the mistress of the house, that having no chest at hand, she had clapped the plaster on a large box in the corner of the sick-chamber.

Dr. Edward Jorden (1569-1632), an English physician, wrote regarding the oftentimes successful results of treatment by means of incantations, and leechdoms or medical formulas, that these measures have no inherent supernatural virtue; but in the words of Avicenna, "the confidence of the patient in the means used is oftentimes more available to cure diseases than all other remedies whatsoever."

From the beginning of time, the fortune-teller, the sorcerer, the interpreter of dreams, the charlatan, the wild medicine-man, the educated physician, the mesmerist, and the hypnotist, have made use of the patient's imagination, to help them in their work. They have all recognized the potency and availability of that force.[63:1]

Modern psychology explains the healing force of verbal charms as being due to the power of suggestion. For these suggest the idea of a cure to the subjective mind, which controls the bodily functions and conditions. Robert Burton, in the "Anatomy of Melancholy," said in reference to this subject:

All the world knows there is no vertue in charms; but a strong conceit and opinion alone, which forceth a motion of the humours, spirits and blood, which takes away the cause of the malady from the parts affected. The like we may say of the magical effects, superstitious cures, and such as are done by mountebanks and wizards. . . . Imagination is the medium deferens of Passions, by whose means they work and produce many times prodigious effects.

To give joy to the sick, said the Latin historian Cassiodorus, is natural healing; for, once make your patient cheerful, and his cure is accomplished. In like vein is an aphorism of Celsus: It is the mark of a skilled practitioner to sit awhile by the bedside, with a blithe countenance.

William Ramesey, M.D., in "Elminthologia" (1668), remarks that fancy doth not only cause but also as easily cureth divers diseases. To this agency may be properly referred many alleged magical and juggling cures, attributed to saints, images, relics, holy waters, avemarys, benedictions, charms, characters, and sigils of the planets. All such cures, wrote this author, are to be ascribed to the force of the imagination.

Written charms against toothache in Christian lands have usually a marked family resemblance; the theme being the same, but the number of variants legion. Saint Peter is represented as afflicted with the toothache, and sitting on a marble stone by the wayside. Our Lord passes by, and cures him by a few spoken words. The following quaintly illiterate version of this spell was in vogue in the north of Scotland within recent years: "Petter was laying his head upon a marrable ston, weping, and Christ came by and said: 'What else [ails] thou, Petter?' Petter answered: 'Lord God, my twoth.' 'Raise thou, Petter, and be healed.' And whosoever shall carry these lines in My Name, shall never feel the twothick."[64:1]

The following is a translation of a Welsh charm against toothache:

"As Peter was sitting alone on a marble stone, Christ came to him and said: 'Peter, what is the matter with you?' 'The toothache, my Lord God.' 'Arise, Peter, and be free'; And every man and woman will be cured of the toothache, who shall believe these words. I do this in the name of God."[65:1]

Another version of this charm is popular in Newfoundland. The inscribed paper, enclosed in a little bag, is hung around the neck of the afflicted person, from whom its contents are carefully concealed. "I've seed it written, a feller was sitten on a marvel stone, and our Lord came by; and he said to him, 'What's the matter with thee, my man?' And he replied, 'Got the toothache, Marster.' Then said our Lord, 'Follow Me, and thee shall have no more toothache.'"[65:2]

Still another form of this spell is in use among Lancashire peasants. The paper, inscribed as follows, is stitched inside the clothing: "Ass Sant Petter sat at the geats of Jerusalm, our Blessed Lord and Sevour Jesus Christ Passed by, and sead, 'What eleth thee?' He sead, 'Lord, my teeth ecketh.' Hee said, 'Arise and follow mee, and thy teeth shall never eake eney mour.' Fiat + Fiat + Fiat."[65:3]

Every one is aware that it is a common experience to have an aversion for certain articles of food, and to be affected unpleasantly by the mere thought of them. Whereas, if a person partakes of such food without knowledge of it, no ill effects may ensue. The sense of taste is affected by the imagination. A man sent the cream from the breakfast-table because it tasted sour, but found it sweet when it was brought back by a servant, supposing it to be a fresh supply. A laxative medicine may produce sleep, in the belief that it is an opiate; and contrariwise, an anodyne may act as a purgative, if the patient believes that it was so intended.[66:1] Dr. Robert T. Edes, in "Mind Cures from the Standpoint of the General Practitioner," remarks that mental action, whether intellectual or emotional, has little or no effect upon certain physiological or pathological processes. Fever, for example, which is such an important symptom of various acute diseases, does not appear to be influenced by the imagination. Typhoid fever runs its course, and is not directly amenable to treatment by suggestion; but nevertheless hope, courage, and an equable mental condition do undoubtedly assist the vis medicatrix natur? The confident expectation of a cure is a powerful factor in bringing it about, doing that which no medical treatment can accomplish.

In recent works on suggestive therapeutics, the curative power of the imagination is emphasized and reiterated. "It is not the faith itself which cures, but faith sets into activity those powers and forces which the unconscious mind possesses over the body, both to cause disease and to cure it."[67:1]

Reference has been made to a certain similitude of religion and superstition. Oftentimes there appears to exist also a remarkable affinity between superstition and rheumatism, for these two are wont to flourish together, as in days of yore. Many a man of intelligence and education has been known to conceal a horse-chestnut in his pocket as an anti-rheumatic charm. A highly respected citizen, of undoubted sanity, was heard to remark that, were he to forget to carry the chestnut which had reposed in his waistcoat pocket for more than twenty years, he should promptly have a recurrence of his ailment.[67:2]

Daniel Hack Tuke, M.D., in referring to the systematic excitement of a definite expectation or hope, in regard to the beneficial action of totally inert substances, relates that a French physician, M. Lisle, especially recognized the efficiency of the imagination as a power in therapeutics. He therefore adopted the method of treating divers ailments by prescribing bread-pills, covered with silver leaf, and labelled pilules argents anti-nerveuses. These pills were eagerly taken by his patients, and the results were highly satisfactory.

We may here appropriately cite one of several cases reported in the "British and Foreign Medical Review," January, 1847. A naval officer had suffered for some years from violent attacks of cramp in the stomach. He had tried almost all the remedies usually recommended for the relief of this troublesome affection. For a short time bismuth had been prescribed, with good results. The attacks came on about once in three weeks, or from that to a month, unless when any unusual exposure brought them on more frequently. Although the bismuth was continued in large doses, it soon lost its effect. Sedatives were given, but the relief afforded by these was only partial, while their effect on the general system was evidently very prejudicial. On one occasion, while suffering from the effect of some preparation of opium, given for the relief of these spasms, he was told that on the next attack he would be given a remedy which was generally believed to be most effective, but which was rarely used, owing to its dangerous qualities. Notwithstanding these, it should be tried, provided he gave his assent. Accordingly, on the next attack, a powder containing four grains of ground biscuit was administered every seven minutes, while the greatest anxiety was expressed, within the patient's hearing, lest too much be given. The fourth dose caused an entire cessation of pain, whereas half-drachm doses of bismuth had never procured the same relief in less than three hours. Four times did the same kind of attack recur, and four times was it met by the same remedy, and with like success! Dr. Tuke remarks that the influence of the mind upon the body, which is ever powerful in health, is equally powerful in disease, and this influence is exceedingly beneficial in aiding the vis medicatrix, and opposing the vis vitiatrix natur?

He dwells upon the remarkable power exerted by the mind "upon any organ or tissue to which the attention is directed, to the exclusion of other ideas, the mind gradually passing into a state in which, at the desire of the operator, portions of the nervous system can be exalted in a remarkable degree, and others proportionately depressed; and thus the vascularity, innervation and function of an organ or tissue can be regulated and modified according to the locality and nature of the disorder. The psychical element in the various methods comprised under psycho-therapeutics, is greatly assisted by physical means, as gentle friction, pointing, passes, et cetera."

At the siege of Breda, in the Netherlands, A. D. 1625, the Prince of Orange, son of William the Silent, availed himself of the "force of imagination" to cure his soldiers during a serious epidemic then prevailing among them. He provided his army surgeons with small vials containing a decoction of wormwood, camomile, and camphor. The troops were informed that a rare and precious remedy had been obtained in the East, with much difficulty and at great expense. Moreover, so great was its potency, that two or three drops in a gallon of water formed a mixture of wonderful therapeutic value. These statements, made with great solemnity, deeply impressed the soldiers, and their expectation of being cured was realized. For we are told that "they took the medicine eagerly, and grew well rapidly."[70:1]

Thomas Fuller, in the "Holy State," book III, chapter 2, relates the following, which he styles a merry example of the power of imagination in relieving fatigue:

"A Gentleman, having led a company of children beyond their usuall journey, they began to be weary, and joyntly cried to him to carry them; which because of their multitude he could not do, but told them he would provide them horses to ride on. Then cutting little wands out of the hedge as nagges for them, and a great stake as a gelding for himself, thus mounted, Phancie put metall into their legs, and they came cheerfully home."

In his ward at the Hital Andral, in Paris, Dr. Mathieu had a large number of tubercular patients. One morning, while making his rounds, he lingered before one of them and remarked to the house physician and the students who were with him:

That there had just been discovered in Germany a specific for tuberculosis-- namely, "antiphymose." Next day he again spoke of this antiphymose, and, in the hearing of the patients, as before, told of the wonderful results it yielded when employed in the treatment of tuberculosis. For a week the patients talked of nothing but that wonderful antiphymose; they couldn't understand why "the chief" didn't try the new drug.

Their wishes were at last acceded to, and the experiments with antiphymose, which Dr. Mathieu said he had obtained from Germany, began. To judge of the action of that drug, which was injected under the skin, it was determined that the house-physician himself should take the temperature and register the weight of the consumptives under treatment.

This was done, and soon it seemed evident that a powerful and highly beneficent medicine was at work. Under the influence of this new remedy, the patients' fever subsided and their weight increased. Some gained a kilogramme and a half, some two, and some even three kilogrammes. Meanwhile the cough ceased, and those who had been unable to touch food began to eat; those who had been unable to sleep now slept all night. And if, to complete the test, the injections of antiphymose were stopped, the fever returned and all the old symptoms reasserted themselves. The victims grew thin.

Now this famous antiphymose, this marvellous drug procured from Germany, was nothing but water, ordinary water, but sterilized in Dr. Mathieu's laboratory! All that talk before the patients about the discovery and therapeutic virtue of antiphymose, all those little bluffs involved in the house-physician's taking the temperature and the weight of the patients, were simply a mise-en-sce designed to create a sort of suggestion and to reinforce it as much as possible. And it was manifestly suggestion, and not the injections of pure water, that checked the fever, arrested the cough, diminished the expectoration, revived the appetite, and increased the weight.[72:1]

A simple experiment, with a view to proving that a patient is accessible to auto-suggestion, is described by Professor Mussterberg. Some interesting-looking apparatus, with a few metal rings, is fastened upon his fingers, and connected with a battery and electric keys. The key is then pushed down in view of the patient, who is instructed to indicate the exact time when he begins to feel the electric current. The sensation will probably shortly be felt in one of his fingers; whereupon the physician can demonstrate to him that there was no connection in the wires, and that the whole galvanic sensation was the result of suggestion.[72:2]

Joseph Jastrow, in "Fact and Fable in Psychology," remarks that the modern forms of irregular healing present apt illustrations of occult methods of treatment which were in vogue long ago. And chief among these is the mental factor, whether utilized when the patient is awake or when he is unconscious, as a curative principle. The legitimate recognition of the importance of mental conditions and influences in therapeutics is one of the results of the union of modern psychology and medicine.

FOOTNOTES:

[53:1] Thomas Jay Hudson, The Law of Psychic Phenomena, p. 23.

[54:1] Christian Healing, p. 14.

[54:2] Ibid., p. 7.

[56:1] Dr. Hugo Magnus, Superstition in Medicine.

[58:1] McClure's Magazine, November, 1909.

[59:1] H. Bernheim, M.D., Suggestive Therapeutics, p. 196.

[60:1] Larousse, tome x, p. 1104.

[60:2] Edward Berdoe, The Healing Art, p. 248.

[61:1] Reuben Post Halleck, Psychology and Psychic Culture, p. 166.

[63:1] Mark Twain, Christian Science, p. 34

[64:1] Proceedings of the Society of Antiquarians of Scotland, 3d Series, vol. iii, p. 492. Edinburgh, 1893.

[65:1] The Academy, vol. xxxi, p. 258; 1887.

[65:2] Journal of American Folk-Lore, vol. viii, p. 287; 1895.

[65:3] John Harland and T. T. Wilkinson, Lancashire Folk-Lore.

[66:1] Alfred T. Schofield, M.D., The Unconscious Mind, p. 288.

[67:1] Alfred T. Schofield, M.D., The Unconscious Mind, p. 366.

[67:2] Boston Herald, February 20, 1909.

[70:1] Adams, The Healing Art, vol. i, p. 202.

[72:1] Dr. R. Romme, in La Revue.

[72:2] Psychotherapy, p. 213.

CHAPTER VI

THE ROYAL TOUCH

Malcolm. Well; more anon.--Comes the king forth, I pray you?

Doctor. Ay, sir; there are a crew of wretched souls That stay his cure: their malady convinces The great assay of art; but at his touch-- Such sanctity hath heaven given his hand-- They presently amend.

Malcolm. I thank you, doctor. [Exit Doctor.

Macduff. What's the disease he means?

Malcolm. 'Tis called the evil: A most miraculous work in this good king; Which often, since my here-remain in England, I have seen him do. How he solicits heaven, Himself best knows: but strangely visited people, All swoln and ulcerous, pitiful to the eye, The mere despair of surgery, he cures, Hanging a golden stamp about their necks, Put on with holy prayers: and 'tis spoken, To the succeeding royalty he leaves The healing benediction. With this strange virtue, He hath a heavenly gift of prophecy, And sundry blessings hang about his throne, That speak him full of grace. Macbeth, Act IV, Scene 3.

The healing of physical ailments by laying-on of hands was in vogue in the earliest historic times. Certain Egyptian sculptures have been found, illustrative of this practice, wherein one of the healer's hands is represented as touching the patient's stomach, and the other as applied to his back.[74:1]

From numerous references to the subject in Holy Writ, three are here given: "Neglect not the gift that is in thee, which was given thee by prophecy, with the laying on of hands of the Presbytery."[74:2] "They shall take up serpents; and if they drink any deadly thing, it shall not hurt them; they shall lay hands on the sick, and they shall recover." "And he could there do no mighty work, save that he laid his hands upon a few sick folk, and healed them."[74:3]

We are told that Asclepiades of Bithynia, a famous Grecian physician of the second century B. C., who practised at Rome, systematically employed the "induced trance" in the treatment of certain affections. Probably he considered this method to conform with certain principles which he advocated. For he professed that a physician's duty consisted in healing his patients safely, speedily, and pleasantly; and as he met with considerable success, his system was naturally very popular. It seems certain that the physicians of old had no true conception of the psychological and physiological principles of healing by laying on of hands. It is probable, on the other hand, that they used this method in a haphazard way, relying largely on the confidence of their patients and the expectation of cure.[75:1]

Tacitus, in his "History," book IV, chapter 81, relates that at the instance of the God Serapis, a citizen of Alexandria, who had a maimed hand, entreated that he might be pressed by the foot and sole of Vespasian (A. D. 9-79). The Emperor at first ridiculed the request, and treated it with disdain. However, upon learning the opinion of physicians that a cure might be effected through the application of a healing power, and that it was the pleasure of the gods that he should be the one to make the attempt, Vespasian, with a cheerful countenance, did what was required of him, while the multitude that stood by awaited the event in all the confidence of anticipated success. Immediately, wrote the historian, the functions of the affected hand were restored.

The priests and magi of the ancient Druids possessed a wonderful faculty of healing. They were able to hypnotize their patients by the waving of a wand, and while under the spell of this procedure, the latter could tell what was happening afar off, being vested with the power of clairvoyance.

But the Druidic priests also effected cures by stroking with the hand, and this method was thought to be of special efficacy in rheumatic affections. They also employed other remedies which appealed to the imagination, such as various mesmeric charms and incantations.[76:1]

John Timbs remarks in "Doctors and Patients," that any person who claimed to possess the special gift of healing, was expected to demonstrate his ability by means of the touch; for this was the established method of testing the genuineness of any assumed or pretended curative powers. Among Eastern nations at the present time, European physicians are popularly credited with the faculty of healing by manual stroking or passes, and the same ideas prevail in remote communities of Great Britain. In the opinion of the author above mentioned, the belief in the transmission of remedial virtues by the hands is derived from the fact that these members are the usual agents in the bestowal of material benefits, as, for example, in almsgiving to the poor.

According to the popular view, royal personages were exalted above other people, "because they possessed a distinctive excellence, imparted to them at the hour of birth by the silent rulers of the night." In view of this belief, it was natural that sovereigns should be invested with extraordinary healing powers, and that they should be enabled, by a touch of the hand, to communicate to others an infinitesimal portion of the virtues with which they had been supernaturally endowed. These virtues dwelt also in the king's robes. Hence arose the belief in the miraculous power of healing by the imposition of royal hands.[77:1]

There is nothing that can cure the King's Evil, But a Prince. JOHN LYLY (1553-1606), Euphues.

The treatment of scrofulous patients by the touch of a reigning sovereign's hand is believed to have originated in France. According to one authority, Clovis I (466-511) was the pioneer in employing this method of cure. Louis I (778-840) is reported to have added thereto the sign of the cross. The custom was in vogue during the reign of Philip I (1051-1108), but that monarch is said to have forfeited the power of healing, by reason of his immorality and profligacy.[77:2] During later medieval times the Royal Touch appears to have fallen into disuse in France, reappearing, however, in the reign of Louis IX (1215-1270), and we have the authority of Laurentius, physician to Henry IV, that Francis I, while a prisoner at Madrid after the battle of Pavia, in 1525, "cured multitudes of people daily of the Evil."

The Royal Touch was a prerogative of the kings of England from before the Norman Conquest until the beginning of the Hanoverian dynasty, a period of nearly seven hundred years, and the custom affords a striking example of the power of the imagination and of popular credulity. The English annalist, Raphael Holinshed, wrote in 1577 concerning King Edward the Confessor (1004-1066), that he had the gift of healing divers ailments, and that "he used to help those that were vexed with the King's Evil, and left that virtue, as it were, a portion of inheritance, unto his successors, the kings of this realm."

But the earliest reference to this king as a healer by the touch was made by the English historian, William of Malmesbury (1095-1143), in his work, "De Gestis Regum Anglorum." The story, wrote Joseph Frank Payne, M.D., in "English Medicine in the Anglo-Saxon Times," has the familiar features of the legends and miracles of healing by the early ecclesiastics, saints, or kings, as they are found in the histories and chronicles from the time of Bede, the Venerable (673-735). But there appears to be no real historical evidence that Edward the Confessor was the first royal personage who healed by laying on of hands.

John Aubrey, in his "Miscellanies," asserts, on the authority of certain English chronicles, that in the reign of King Henry III (1206-1272), there lived a child who was endowed with the gift of healing, and whose touch cured many diseases. Popular belief, as is well known, ascribed this prerogative also to a seventh son.

Pettigrew, in his "Superstitions connected with the History and Practice of Medicine and Surgery," said that Gilbertus Anglicus, the author of a "Compendium Medicin?" and the first practical writer on medicine in Britain, who is believed to have flourished in the time of Edward I (1239-1307), asserted that the custom of healing by the Royal Touch was an ancient one.

In the opinion of William George Black ("Folk-Medicine," 1883), the subject belongs rather to the domain of history than to that of popular superstitions.

Thomas Bradwardin, an eminent English prelate of the fourteenth century, and Archbishop of Canterbury, described the usage in question as already long-established in his time; and Sir John Fortescue, Lord Chief Justice of England, during Henry the Sixth's reign, declared that the English kings had exercised this privilege from time immemorial.

In a small tract published by His Majesty's command, entitled, "The Ceremonies for the Healing of them that be diseased with the King's Evil, used in the Time of King Henry VII" (1456-1509), we find that it was customary for the patients to kneel before the king during the religious exercises, which were conducted by the chaplain. After laying his hands upon them, the monarch crossed the affected portion of the body of each patient with an "Angel of Gold Noble." This coin bore as its device the archangel Michael, standing upon and piercing a dragon. In later reigns it was replaced by a small golden or silver medal, having the same emblem, and known as a touch-piece.

Andrew Borde, in his "Breviary of Health" (1547, the last year of the reign of Henry VIII), in reference to the King's Evil, wrote as follows: "For this matter, let every man make friendes to the Kynges Majestie, for it doth perteyne to a Kynge to helpe this infirmitie, by the grace of God, the which is geven to a king anoynted. But forasmuch as some men doth judge divers times a fystle or a French pocke to be the king's evill, in such matters it behoveth not a kynge to medle withall."

Queen Elizabeth, who reigned from 1558 to 1603, continued the practice, as we are informed by her chaplain, Rev. Dr. William Tooker, who published in 1590 a quarto volume on the subject, in which he claimed that the power of healing by touch had been exercised by royal personages from a very early period. He asserted that the Queen never refused touching any one who applied for relief, if, upon examination by her medical advisers, the applicant was found to be affected with the King's Evil. The Queen was especially disposed to touch indigent persons, who were unable to pay for private treatment. Although averse to the practice, Queen Elizabeth continued to exercise the prerogative, doubtless from philanthropic motives, and in deference to the popular wish. William Clowes, an eminent contemporary practitioner, and chief surgeon of Bartholomew's Hospital, London, in a monograph issued in 1602, wrote that the struma or evill was known to be "miraculously healed by the sacred hands of the Queene's most royall majesty, even by divine inspiration and wonderfull worke and power of God, above man's skill, arte and expectation."[81:1]

When, in 1603, on the death of Elizabeth, James VI of Scotland became King of England with the title of James I, he was sceptical regarding the efficacy of the Royal Touch. The Scotch ministers, whom he brought with him, urged its abandonment as a superstitious ceremony; while his English counsellors recommended its continuance, maintaining that a failure so to do would amount to a debasing of royalty. Unwillingly therefore he followed the advice of the latter.

We do not find many references to the prevalence of this custom in the reign of Charles I, but there is evidence that it was in use at that time. This is apparent in certain extracts from State Papers, relating chiefly to medicine and pharmacy, published under the direction of the Master of the Rolls, as follows:

April 10, 1631. John, Lord Poulett, sent a child, a little girl, to the King, to be touched for the King's Evil, and she has come home safely, and mends every day in health.

January 15, 1632. Godre, Bois, a Frenchman, prisoner in the King's Bench, takes upon him to cure the King's Evil, and daily a great concourse of people flocked to him, although it is conceived that if such cures have been, it is rather by sorcery and incantation than by any skill he has in physic. Endorsed: The Lord Chief Justice of the King's Bench is to call him for examination, to be indicted for cosenage.

June 7, 1632. Sir Thomas Richardson, Lord Chief Justice of the King's Bench, to the Council, thinks there is not sufficient evidence to convict Bois Gaudre of cosenage or sorcery, but thinks he has committed a contempt worth punishment, in taking upon him to cure the King's Evil. He has imprisoned him, of which he complains bitterly.

June 7, 1632. Examination of James Philip Gaudre, Knight of St. Lazare, in France. Is a Frenchman, and has been in England for seven years, chiefly at Sir Thomas Wolseley's house, whose daughter he married, until two years past, he was arrested for debt. By his experience in surgery, has recovered many poor persons of the King's Evil, some before His Majesty touched them, and some after. Never made any benefit by his skill, other than sometimes those whom he had done good to would give him a Capon, or small sums paid by him for herbs and other things. Used his skill often in France, and cured many. Did not cure any in England until Midsummer last, when a poor man, who had but one son, who was sick of that disease, made moan to him, and he cured him. Thinks that by reason he is the youngest of seven sons, he performs that cure with better success than others, except the King. Has no skill in sorcery, witchcraft, or enchantment, nor ever used any such thing.[82:1]

The ceremony of the Royal Touch reached its height of popularity during the reign of Charles II (1630-1685). From the "Diary of John Evelyn," we learn that His Majesty began to touch for the King's Evil, July 6, 1660. The King sat in state, attended by the surgeons and the Lord Chamberlain. The opening prayers and the Gospel having been read, the patients knelt on the steps of the throne, and were stroked on either cheek by the King's hand, the chaplain saying: "He put his hands upon them and healed them." Then the King hung a gold "angel" around the neck of each one. On March 28, 1684, so great was the concourse of people, with their children, anxious to be cured, that six or seven were crushed to death "by pressing at the Chirurgeon's door for tickets."

Dr. Richard Wiseman, favorite surgeon of Charles II, wrote that a belief in the Royal Touch was evidently a party tenet. It was therefore encouraged by the sovereign, and upheld by all who were disposed to please the Court. In commenting on the alleged efficacy of this treatment, Dr. Wiseman expressed his conviction that the imagination of the patient was doubtless powerfully affected by the magnificence and splendor of the ceremony. Failure to receive benefit was ascribed to lack of faith. It was said that Charles once handled a scrofulous Quaker with such vigor, that he made him a healthy man and a sound Churchman in a moment.[83:1]

Women quacks were very numerous at this period, and throve exceedingly. Their resoluteness in thrusting their ignorant pretensions upon the public, gave evidence of the same dogged pertinacity which characterizes the modern suffragettes in their fanatical efforts to obtain redress for alleged wrongs.

Thus the psychic healing forces are ever potent, so long as the patient has faith in the treatment employed.

Dr. John Browne, a surgeon in ordinary to Charles II, published a treatise entitled "Charisma Basilicon, or the royal gift of healing strumas, or king's-evil swellings, by contact or imposition of the sacred hands of our kings of England and France, given them at their inaugurations."

The elaborate ceremonies and the presentation of gold pieces were regarded by the author as evidences of the great piety, charity, and humility of the sovereign. He comments moreover on the admirable results of this treatment among people of many nationalities.

None ever hitherto mist thereof, wrote he, unless their little faith and incredulity starved their merits, or they received his gracious hand for curing another disease, which was not really allowed to be cured by him; and as bright evidences hereof, I have presumed to offer that some have immediately upon the very touch been cured; others not so easily, till the favour of a second repetition thereof.

Some also, losing their gold, their diseases have seized them afresh, and no sooner have these obtained a second touch and new gold, but their diseases have been seen to vanish, as being afraid of his majestie's presence.[85:1]

Of the vast numbers of patients who repaired to the healing receptions of Charles II, doubtless many were attracted by curiosity, and others by the desire for gold.

In the Parliamentary Journal for July 2-9, 1660, it was stated that the kingdom having been for a long time troubled with the evil, by reason of His Majesty's absence, great numbers have lately flocked for cure.

His sacred majesty, on Monday last, touched 250, in the banquetting house; among whom, when his majesty was delivering the gold, one shuffled himself in, out of an hope of profit, which had not been stroked; but his majesty quickly discovered him, saying: "this man hath not yet been touched." His majesty hath, for the future, appointed every Friday for the cure, at which 200, and no more, are to be presented to him, who are first to repair to Mr. Knight, the king's surgeon, being at the Cross Guns, in Russell Street, Covent Garden, over against the Rose Tavern, for their tickets.

The presentation of the gold was regarded as a token of the king's good will, and a pledge of his wish for the patient's recovery. Silver coins were sometimes used, but the sovereign power of gold was distinctly admitted, as the disease is reported to have returned, in some cases, upon the medal being lost. The presentation of a second golden touch-piece was alleged to be effective in subduing the scrofula.

The following announcement appeared in the "Public Intelligencer," under date of Whitehall, May 14, 1664:

"His Sacred Majesty, having declared it to be his Royal will and purpose to continue the healing of his People for the Evil during the month of May, and then to give over till Michaelmas next, I am commanded to give notice thereof, that the people may not come up to Town in the interim and lose their labour."

Charles II is said to have found the practice extremely lucrative. It is not surprising that many practitioners in those days were credited with having wrought marvellous cures.

We know that the undoubted influence of the mind on the body, and the power of suggestion and expectant attention, apply only to subjective states and functional ailments. Thus it is intelligible why so many people of education and culture, on the principle that seeing is believing, were able to testify to miraculous cures in their own experience.[86:1]

William Andrews, in "Historic Romance," says that the records of the Town of Preston, Lancashire, show that the local Corporation voted grants of money to enable patients to make the journey to London, to be touched for the evil. In the year 1682 bailiffs were instructed to "pay unto James Harrison, bricklayer, ten shillings, towards carrying his son to London, in order to the procuring of His Majesty's touch." Again, in 1687, being the third year of James II, when the King was at Chester, the Preston Town Council passed a vote, ordering the payment to two young women, of five shillings each, "towards their charge in going to Chester to get His Majesty's touch."

Thomas Cartwright, Bishop of Chester, wrote in his diary, August 27, 1687: "I was at His Majesty's levee, from whence, at nine o'clock, I attended him into the closet, where he healed three hundred and fifty persons."

Queen Anne (1702-1714) was the last of the English sovereigns who exercised the royal prerogative of healing by laying-on of hands. She made an official announcement in the London "Gazette," March 12, 1712, of her intention to "touch publicly." Samuel Johnson, then a child of about three years of age, was one of the last who tested the efficacy of this superstitious rite, and without success. Acting upon the advice of Sir John Floyer, a noted physician of Lichfield, Mrs. Johnson took her son to London, where he was touched by the Queen. When asked in later years if he could remember the latter, he used to say that he had a "confused, but somehow a sort of solemn recollection of a lady in diamonds and a long black hood."[88:1] George I, the successor of Queen Anne, regarded the Royal Touch as a purely superstitious method of healing, and during his reign the practice fell into desuetude.

The English jurist, Daines Barrington (1727-1800), in his "Observations upon the Statutes," relates the case of an old man whom he was examining as a witness. This man stated that he had been touched for the evil by Queen Anne, when she was at Oxford. Upon being asked whether the treatment had been effective, he replied facetiously that he did not believe that he ever had the evil, but that his parents were poor, and did not object to the piece of gold.[88:2]

During the reign of George II, a writer of a speculative turn of mind queried whether the disuse of this long-established custom might be attributed to the sullenness of the reigning prince, who, as was generally known, had received many evidences of his subjects' displeasure; or whether the alleged divine power of healing by the Royal Touch had been withdrawn from him. And it was replied that the sovereign had as good a title as any of his predecessors to perform this holy operation. Moreover, he was so much in love with all sorts of pageantry and acts of power that he would willingly do his part. But the degeneracy and wickedness of the times, which tended to bring all pious and holy things into contempt, and then into disuse, was the reason for this neglect.[89:1]

In the year 1746, or thereabouts, one Christopher Lovel, a native of Wells, in Somersetshire, but afterwards a resident of Bristol, being sadly afflicted with the King's Evil, and having during many years made trial of all the remedies which medical science could suggest, and without any effect, decided to go abroad in search of a cure. Proceeding to France, he was touched at Avignon by the eldest lineal descendant of a race of kings, who had, for a long succession of ages, healed by exercising the royal prerogative. But this descendant and heir had not at that time been crowned. Notwithstanding this fact, however, the usual effects followed, and from the moment that the man was touched, and invested with the narrow ribbon, to which a small silver coin was pendant, according to the rites prescribed in the office appointed by the Church for that solemnity, he began to mend, and recovered strength daily, arriving at Bristol in good health, after an absence of some four months.

Such, briefly, is an account of this remarkable case, as given in Thomas Carte's "History of England," published about 1746. But a contributor to the "Gentleman's Magazine," January 13, 1747, who signed himself Amicus Veritatis, wrote in reference to the foregoing account, expressing surprise that sensible people should give credit to such a tale, which was calculated to support the old threadbare notion of the divine hereditary right of royal personages to cure by touch. The then reigning sovereign, George II, wrote he, despised such childish delusions.

The report of this alleged wonderful case made a great noise among the ignorant classes. But the sceptic writer above mentioned argued that Lovel's cure was but temporary, and that the benefit was due to change of air and a strict regimen, rather than to the touch of the Pretender's hand at Avignon. For, queried he, can any man with a grain of reason believe that such an idle, superstitious charm as the touch of a man's hand can convey a virtue sufficiently efficacious to heal so stubborn a disorder as the King's Evil?

French tradition ascribes the origin of the gift of healing by royal touch, to Saint Marculf, a monk whose Frankish ancestry is shown by his name, which signifies forest wolf. This personage was a native of Bayeux, and is reputed to have flourished in the sixth century A. D. His relics were preserved in an abbey at Corbigny, and thither the French monarchs were accustomed to resort, after their coronation at Rheims, to obtain the pretended power of curing the King's Evil, by touching the relics of this saint. But according to the historian, Francis Eudes de Meray (1610-1683), the gift was bestowed upon King Clovis (466-511) at the time of his baptism.

In 1515, the year of his accession, Francis I laid his hands on a number of persons in the presence of the Pope, during the prevalence of an epidemic at Bologna, Italy. And in 1542 he issued the following statement: "On our return from Rheims, we went to Corbigny, where we and our predecessors have been accustomed to make oblations, and pay reverence to the precious relics of Saint Marculf for the admirable gift of healing the King's Evil, which he imparted miraculously to the kings of France, at the pleasure of the Creator. The grace we exercised in the usual way, by touching the parts affected, and signing them with the sign of the cross."

Louis XIII of France (1601-1643) is said to have bestowed upon Cardinal Richelieu all of his prerogatives, except the Royal Touch.

His successor, Louis the Great, is credited with having touched sixteen hundred people on Easter Sunday, 1686, using the words, "Le Roy te touche, Dieu te guisse." Every French patient received a present of fifteen sous, while foreigners were given double that amount.[91:1]

According to the Swiss theologian, Samuel Werenfels (1657-1740), who published a treatise on "The Power of curing the King's Evil," this prerogative was shared by the members of the House of Hapsburg. And the same authority relates that the kings of Hungary were able to heal various affections by the Royal Touch, and to neutralize by this method the toxic effects of the bite of venomous creatures.

FOOTNOTES:

[74:1] Joseph Ennemoser, The History of Magic, vol. i, p. 209.

[74:2] 1 Timothy, iv, 14.

[74:3] Mark, xvi, 18; vi, 5.

[75:1] H. Addington Bruce, in The Outlook, September, 1909.

[76:1] Lady Wilde, Ancient Cures, Charms, and Usages of Ireland.

[77:1] J. Cordy Jeaffreson, A Book about Doctors.

[77:2] Chambers's Encyclopedia.

[81:1] Pettigrew, op. cit., p. 132.

[82:1] John Morgan Richards, A Chronology of Medicine.

[83:1] Lord Macaulay, The History of England, vol. iii, p. 379.

[85:1] Thomas Joseph Pettigrew, Medical Superstitions.

[86:1] The Lancet, vol. ii, 1901.

[88:1] Once a Week, vol. xv (1866), p. 219.

[88:2] E. Cobham Brewer, A Dictionary of Miracles.

[89:1] Common-sense, August 13, 1737.

[91:1] Hon. Daines Barrington, Observations upon the Statutes, 1766.

CHAPTER VII

THE BLUE-GLASS MANIA

As illustrative of the power of the imagination, the so-called blue-glass mania, which prevailed extensively in this country, affords a striking example. About the year 1868, General Augustus J. Pleasanton, of Philadelphia, made some experiments to determine whether or not rays of sunlight passing through colored glass had any therapeutic effect on animals and plants. His selection of blue glass as a medium was probably based upon the theory that the blue ray of the solar spectrum possesses superior actinic or chemical properties.

Experimenting first on plants, he adopted the method of inserting panes of blue and violet glass in the roof of his grapery, and noticed as a result an apparent extraordinary rapidity and luxuriance of growth of the vines, and later a correspondingly large harvest of grapes. Encouraged by this success, he built a piggery, having a glass roof, of which one portion was fitted with panes of blue glass, and the other with ordinary transparent glass. It was claimed that the pigs kept under the former developed more rapidly than those under the latter. An Alderney bull-calf, which was very small and feeble at birth, was placed in a pen under violet glass. In twenty-four hours it was able to walk and became quite animated. By the same method a mule was reported to have been cured of obstinate rheumatism and deafness. Again, a canary-bird, which had been an exceptionally fine warbler, declined to eat or sing, and appeared to be in a feeble state of health. The bird in its cage was placed in the bath-room of its owner's dwelling, the windows of which contained colored-glass panes. It was alleged that the little creature speedily improved; its voice became sweeter and more melodious than ever, while its appetite was simply voracious.

Notable cures of human beings were also reported. Cases of neuralgia and rheumatism were said to have been benefited, the development of young infants vastly promoted, while as a tonic for producing hair on bald heads, blue glass was a veritable specific. During the year 1877 popular interest in the craze reached its culmination. In this country the furore assumed national proportions. Peddlers went from door to door in the cities, selling blue glass, and did a thriving business; while many instances of remarkable cures effected by the new panacea were recorded in the newspapers. Then after a time came the reaction; the whole theory became a subject for ridicule and satire, and the public mind was ready to turn its attention to some other fad.

But in spite of the fickleness of the popular mind, this well-known fact remains, that a good sun-bath, with or without the medium of colored glass, is often of great hygienic value. There is truth in the Italian proverb: Dove non va il sole, va il medico: where the sunlight enters not, there goes the physician.

I have thus attempted briefly to describe the blue-glass mania, because it seems aptly to illustrate the healing force of the imagination. So long as people have confidence in blue glass and sunlight combined, to cure fleshly ills, these agents undoubtedly act in many cases "like a charm," and may be classed as mental curatives.

In recent years, however, efforts have been made to determine whether certain colored rays of the spectrum were more potent than others therapeutically. Under the caption "Light-Cures, Old and New," in "Everybody's Magazine," October, 1902, Arthur E. Bostwick, Ph.D., remarks that there was a germ of truth in the blue-glass craze, for it has recently been shown that the red rays are injuriously stimulative in eruptive diseases, and of course the blue glass strained these rays out. It goes without saying that if there were simply health-giving qualities in the blue rays and no injurious ones in the red and yellow, ordinary light would be as effective as that which had passed through blue glass; for the glass introduces no new quality or color into the light; it only absorbs certain rays of the spectrum, allowing others to pass. If blue light, therefore, is more healthful than white, it must be because the remainder of the spectrum has an injurious effect.

An Austrian physician, Dr. Kaiser, has recently asserted, in a paper read before the Vienna Medical Society, that blue light is effective in reducing inflammation, allaying pain, and curing skin-disease, especially by promoting absorption of morbid humors. He asserts that a beam from a powerful lantern, after passing through blue glass, will kill cultures of various bacilli, when directed upon them at a distance of fifteen feet for half an hour daily during six days.

CHAPTER VIII

THE TEMPLES OF ESCULAPIUS

It has been truly said that temples were the first hospitals, and priests the earliest physicians.[97:1] In the temples of Esculapius, in Greece, a main object of the various mystic rites was to exert a powerful influence on the patient's imagination. This was supplemented by practical therapeutic and hygienic treatment, such as baths, friction of the skin, and a strict diet. These primitive sanatoria were built in places carefully chosen for their salubrity of climate and healthful environment. Doubtless their founders were actuated by a belief that Esculapius was ever ready to help those who first helped themselves. In view, therefore, of the superior hygienic conditions, together with intelligent medical care, it is not surprising that seemingly marvellous cures should result, especially of impressionable persons affected with nervous disorders.

The walls of those temples were adorned with bas-reliefs, of which specimens have been preserved. One of these represents a recumbent patient, and a physician seated by the bedside. Near by stands a tall, erect personage, supposed to be the god of health, while the figures of two suppliants may be seen approaching him.[98:1] When a patient arrived at the gate of the temple, he was not allowed to enter at once; for strict cleanliness was deemed a prerequisite for admission to the god's presence. And in order to place him in this desirable condition with the greatest possible despatch, he was plunged into cold water, after which he was permitted to enter the sacred precincts. According to a poetic fancy of the Grecian pilgrim in search of health, the proper cure for his ailment would be revealed by the god of healing to his worshipper in the latter's dreams.[98:2] The interpretation of these dreams and the revelation to the patient of their alleged meaning was entrusted to a priest, who served as an intermediary between Esculapius and the patient. Several of these oracular prescriptions, inscribed upon a marble slab, were found on the site of an Esculapian temple near Rome. Translations of two of them may serve as examples:

"Lucius, having a pleurisy, and being given over by everybody, received from the god this oracle, that he should come and take the ashes off his altar, and mixing them with wine, apply them to his side. Which done, he was cured, and returned thanks to the god, and the people congratulated him upon his happy recovery."

"The god gave this oracle to a blind soldier, named Valerius Aper, that he should mingle the blood of a white cock with honey, and make a collyrium, which he should put upon his eyes three days together. After which he saw, and came publicly to return thanks."[99:1]

Although usually regarded as a purely mythological being, Esculapius is believed by some writers to have been an historic personage. According to tradition, he transmitted his professional knowledge to his descendants, the Asclepiad? a priestly caste, versed in medical lore. For centuries the most famous Grecian physicians were members of this order; and the great Hippocrates, styled "the Father of Medicine," is said to have claimed to be the seventeenth in direct descent from Esculapius.[99:2] Although the god of healing may be said to have been also the first practising physician, his distinguished teacher Chiron, the wise Centaur, was without doubt the first medical professor whose name has been handed down. To Chiron is usually ascribed the honor of having introduced among the Grecians the art of Medicine, in the thirteenth century B. C. He was reputed to have been a learned chief or prince of Thessaly, who was also a pioneer among equestrians, one who preferred horseback as a means of locomotion, rather than the chariot, or other prototype of the chaise, buggy, automobile, or bicycle. Hence the superstition of that rude age gave him a place among the Centaurs. He is reported moreover to have imparted instruction to the Argonauts, and to the warriors who participated in the siege of Troy. From this hero is derived the name of the plant centaury, owing to a legend of its having been used with success as a healing application to a wound in Chiron's foot.

The worship of Esculapius, as the god of healing, was widespread among the Greeks, and lasted even into Christian times. Patients repaired to the temples, just as relief is sought to-day by a devotional pilgrimage, or by a resort to a sacred spring. The records of cures were inscribed upon the columns or walls of the temple, and thus is believed to have originated the custom of recording medical and surgical cases.[100:1]

The priests exerted a powerful influence upon the minds of applicants by reciting wonderful tales, as they led them through the sacred precincts, explaining in mystical language the miraculous cures which had been performed there, and calling attention to the numerous votive offerings and inscriptions upon the temple walls. It may readily be conceived, wrote Richard J. Dunglison, M.D.,[100:2] that these procedures made a deep impression upon the patients' minds, and the more so, because the priests were wont to dwell especially upon the cures which had been effected in analogous cases.

Moreover hydro-therapy was supplemented by massage, which often had beneficial results in nervous affections; and fumigation of the patients, before they received advice from the oracle, lent an air of mystery. Those who were cured returned to express their gratitude and to offer presents to the god, as well as to the priests. They usually also brought some ornament for the adornment of the temple.

The act of sleeping in a sanctuary, in order to obtain medical relief, either through revelations by dreams, or through a divine visitation, was termed incubation.

According to the philosophy of oneiromancy, or the art of taking omens from dreams, during sleep the soul was released from the body, and thus enabled to soar into spiritual regions and commune with celestial beings. Therefore memories of ideas suggested in dreams were cherished as divine revelations.[101:1]

The opinion has been advanced that the methods employed to procure "temple sleep" were similar to those in use at the present time for the production of the hypnotic state. A cure was effected by awakening a healing instinct in the patient's subconscious mind.[101:2]

So far as we are aware, no authentic rational explanation has been given of the phenomenal appearance of a god in the patient's presence. It seems plausible that Asklepios, the Grecian Esculapius, was personated by some priest of majestic mien, who gave oracular medical advice, which serves as a powerful therapeutic suggestion. Various attendant circumstances doubtless contributed to impress the patient's highly wrought imagination, such as the dim light, the sense of mystery, and, it may be, certain tricks of ventriloquism.

In the earliest days of temple-sleep, that is, probably about the seventh century B. C., this mode of treatment was practised without a tinge of superstition, the applicants' faith being deep and sincere. For in that era the belief was general that human art was powerless to cure disease, and the gods alone could furnish aid. Temple-sleep, wrote Dr. Hugo Magnus, was not degraded into superstition until the physicians had come to the conclusion that the phenomena of disease were not evidence of divine displeasure, but that they were due to natural causes. When therefore this new belief became established, temple-sleep degenerated into a superstitious rite. As early as the fifth century B. C., the celebrated poet, Aristophanes, in his comedy, "Plutus," severely criticized this ceremony, as practised in his time. And, although the more enlightened among the Greeks came to regard it with disfavor, the custom was never entirely abandoned by the ancient world.

Having bathed Plutus in the sea, says the servant Cario, we went to the temple of Esculapius; and when our wafers and preparatory sacrifices were offered on the altar, and our cakes on the flame of Vulcan, we laid him on a couch, as was proper, and made ready our own mattresses. When the priest had extinguished the lights, he told us to go to sleep, adding that if any of us heard the hissing we should by no means stir. We therefore all remained in bed, and made no noise. As for myself, I could not sleep, on account of the odor of a basin of savory porridge which an old woman had at the side of her bed, and which I longed for amazingly. Being, therefore, anxious to creep near it, I raised my head and saw the sacristan take the cakes and dried figs from the sacred table, and going the round of the altars, put all that he could find into a bag. It occurred to me that it would be meritorious in me to follow his example, so I arose to secure the basin of porridge, fearing only that the priest might get at it before me, with his garlands on. . . . The old woman, on hearing me, stretched forth her hand. But I hissed, and seized her fingers with my teeth, as if I were an Esculapian snake; then, drawing back her hand again, she lay down and wrapped herself up quickly, while I swallowed the porridge, and, when full, retired to rest.

The surprising cures frequently effected were inexplicable, even to the scientific minds of antiquity.

Victor Duruy, in his "History of Rome,"[103:1] relates the following instance, on the authority of the Greek writer. A man named Euphronios, who had been an ardent follower of Epicurus, suffered from some obstinate affection which his physicians failed to cure. His relatives therefore carried him into a neighboring Esculapian temple, where in the night, during sleep, he heard the voice of an oracle, saying, "In the case of this man, there is only one means of restoration, namely, to burn the hooks of Epicurus, to knead these sacrilegious ashes with wax, and to cover the stomach and chest with the compound." These directions were carried out, and Euphronios was promptly cured and converted.

FOOTNOTES:

[97:1] J. B. Thiers, Trait?des Superstitions, p. 385.

[98:1] Archives gales de Medecine, November, 1891, pp. 582 et seq.

[98:2] Frank Granger, The Worship of the Romans, p. 158.

[99:1] Daniel Le Clerc, The History of Physic, p. 84.

[99:2] Le Clerc, p. 109.

[100:1] Encyclopedia Britannica, art. "Medicine."

[100:2] History of Medicine.

[101:1] Mary Hamilton, Incubation in Pagan Temples.

[101:2] Dr. Carl du Prel, Die Mystik der alten Griechen; Leipzig, 1888.

[103:1] Vol. vi, p. 399.

CHAPTER IX

STYPTIC CHARMS

Fancy can save or kill; it hath closed up wounds, when the balsam could not, and without the aid of salves, to think hath been a cure. CARTWRIGHT.

With bandage firm Ulysses' knee they bound; Then, chanting mystic lays, the closing wound Of sacred melody confessed the force; The tides of life regained their azure course. The Odyssey, XIX, 535.

Probably the stanching of blood sometimes ascribed to the power of a verbal charm should be accredited to the vis medicatrix of Dame Nature herself. The mere sight of blood, as well as its loss, may induce syncope, a condition favorable to the cessation of hemorrhage. Where faith in a magic spell is strong, it is conceivable that a psychic or emotional force should influence the circulation of the blood, and affect its flow locally by a contraction or dilatation of the arterioles, through the agency of the vaso-motor nerves. Familiar instances are to be seen in the sudden glow or pallor of the cheek, under the stress of intense emotion.

In a curious English manuscript, thought to be of the fourteenth century, which is preserved in the Royal Library at Stockholm, are to be found many specimens of healing-spells; and among them one which was to be repeated in church, as follows: "Here bygynyth a charme for to staunch ye blood. In nomine Patris, etc. Whanne oure Lord was don on ye crosse yane come Longeus thedyr and smot hym yt a spere in hys syde. Blod and water yer come owte at ye wonde, and he wyppyd hys eyne and anon he sawgh kyth thorowgh ye vertu of yat God. Yerfore I conjure the blood yat yu come not oute of yis christen woman. In nomine Patris et Filii," etc.[106:1]

The following "Charme to Stanch Blood" is taken from a manuscript of the fifteenth century: "Jesus, that was in Bethlehem born, and baptyzed was in the flumen Jordane; as stente the water at hys comyng so stente the blood of this man N. thy serwaunt, throw the virtu of thy holy name, Jesu, and of thy cosyn, swete sente Jon. And sey thys Charme fyve tymes, with fyve Pater Nostirs, in the worship of the fyve woundys."

A popular medieval narrative charm for healing wounds and arresting hemorrhage, is to be found in the "Compendium Medicin? of Gilbertus Anglicus, physician to the Archbishop of Canterbury toward the close of the twelfth century. The work was first published at Lyons, France, in the year of 1500.

"Write a cross of Christ, and sing thrice over the place these words, and a Pater Noster: Longinus miles lancea punxit Dominum, et restitit sanguis et recessit dolor."

Longinus or Longeus is the traditional name of the Roman soldier who pierced with a spear the side of our Lord, upon the Cross.[107:1]

Verbal styptic charms were much in vogue among the Irish people in early times. Translations of two such charms may serve as examples. "A child was baptized in the river Jordan; and the water was dark and muddy, but the child was pure and beautiful." These words were repeated over the wound, a finger being placed on the site of the hemorrhage; and then: "In the name of God, and of the Lord Christ, let the blood be stanched."

Another similar charm was as follows:

"There came a man from Bethlehem to be baptised in the river Jordan; but the water was so muddy that it stopped flowing: So let the blood! Let it stop flowing in the name of Jesus, and by the power of Christ!"[107:2]

Homer tells in the Odyssey how the sons of Autolycus cured Ulysses, who had been injured while hunting the wild boar, by stanching the blood flowing from a wound in his leg, by means of a verbal charm. "With nicest care the skilful artists bound the brave, divine Ulysses' ghastly wound; and th' incantations stanch'd the gushing blood."[108:1] We have also the testimony of the Grecian lexicographer, Suidas, that various maladies were cured by the repetition of certain words, in the time of Minos, King of Crete.

In Sir Walter Scott's "Lay of the Last Minstrel," there are frequent references to the use of curative spells; as for example in the following lines:

She drew the splinter from the wound, And with a charm she stanch'd the blood.[108:2]

Again, in "Waverley," the hero of that name, while on a stag hunt with some Scottish chieftains, had the misfortune to sprain an ankle. The venerable Highlander, who officiated as surgeon, proceeded to treat the injury with much ceremony. He first prepared a fomentation by boiling certain herbs which had been gathered at the time of a full moon, a charm being recited the while, of which the following is a translation: "Hail to thee, thou holy herb, that sprung on holy ground! All in the Mount Olivet, first wert thou found. Thou art boot for many a bruise, and healest many a wound; in our Lady's blessed name, I take thee from the ground."

The leech next applied the lotion to Waverley's ankle, at the same time murmuring an incantation; and to this latter procedure, rather than to the medicinal virtue of the herbs, the subsequent alleviation of pain and swelling was attributed by all who were present.

In the rugged, mountainous districts of western Ireland, a region inhabited mostly by shepherds and fishermen, medical practice still devolves largely upon "fairy-women" and "witch-doctors," who rely upon herbs, prayers, and incantations in their treatment of the sick. In Ireland, too, are individuals reputed to be masters of the art of "setting" charms for controlling hemorrhage; their method being the repetition of certain words arbitrarily selected, whose weirdness tends to impress the patient with a sense of the mysterious.[109:1]

Spells for checking the flow of blood are plentiful in the early literature of

Germany, and are still employed to some extent. In Dr. G. Lammert's "Volksmedizin in Bayern" (Walzburg, 1869), many hemostatic formulas are given, which are popular among the peasantry in various portions of the empire. They are usually adjurations or commands addressed to the blood, considered as a personality. Thus a spell in vogue in the mountainous region of Odenwald in Hesse, is as follows: "Blood, stand still, as Christ stood still in the river Jordan."

In "Folk-Lore," March, 1908, reference is made to a styptic spell in use at the present time in northern Devonshire, among wise women who are skilled in the art of controlling hemorrhage by psychic methods. The spell consists in repeating the verse, Ezekiel, XVI, 6. In the locality above mentioned it is customary to seek the aid of one of these professional "stenters," instead of a surgeon or veterinarian, and the people have implicit faith in this mode of treatment. The presence of the wise woman is not essential. She merely pronounces the spell wherever she may happen to be, with the assurance that it will be found effectual, on the return of the messenger to the patient.

The prevalence of similar beliefs is shown in the following verse from a popular poem of the seventeenth century:

Tom Pots was but a serving-man; But yet he was a Doctor good; He bound his kerchief on the wound, And with some kind words stanch'd the blood.

FOOTNOTES:

[106:1] Archeologia, vol. xxx, p. 401; 1844.

[107:1] J. F. Payne, M.D., English Medicine in the Anglo-Saxon Times.

[107:2] Lady Wilde, Ancient Cures, Charms, and Usages of Ireland.

[108:1] This is the earliest mention of a medical charm in classic literature, and hence originated the phrase "Homeric Cure," as applied to healing by magical verses.

[108:2] Canto III, section xxiii.

CHAPTER X

HEALING-SPELLS IN ANCIENT TIMES

Neither doth fansy only cause, but also as easily cure diseases; as I may justly refer all magical cures thereunto, performed, as is thought, by saints, images, relicts, holy waters, shrines, avemarys, crucifixes, benedictions, charms, characters, sigils of the planets, inverted words, etc. And therefore all such cures are rather to be ascribed to the force of the imagination, than to any virtue in themselves. RAMESEY, Elminthologia: 1668.

His night-spell is his guard, and charms his physicians. BISHOP HALL, Characters of Vertues and Vices.

Certain Chaldean and Persian words were formerly believed to have a particular efficacy against the demons of sickness. The languages of men, it was averred, were not of human origin, but were gifts from the gods; and inasmuch as magic had its source in Chaldea and other Eastern countries, it was reasoned that certain words of the languages spoken in those places were possessed of an inherent magical value.[111:1] Hence these words were used in invocations addressed to spirits. In the popular belief of the ancient Babylonians, illnesses were caused by the entrance into the body of divers aerial spirits, and incantations were the chief means employed for their expulsion.

In Accadian medical magic, on the same principle, bedridden patients were treated by fastening about their heads "sentences from a good book."[112:1] Naturally, among nations where such views prevailed, physicians were but little esteemed, and the cure of disease devolved upon exorcists and sorcerers. Medicine was merely a branch of Magic, and not a rational science, as in more enlightened countries. Incantations against the spirits of disease were usually recited by the priests, who were supposed, by reason of their education and training, to be specially expert in the choice of the most efficient formulas.

The Chaldean medical amulets were of various kinds. Frequently they consisted of precious stones, engraved with mystic sentences; or strips of cloth, upon which were written talismanic verses, after the manner of Jewish phylacteries. But of whatever form, the chief source of their supposed efficacy appears to have been the words and characters inscribed upon them.[112:2] Gradually, however, a system of therapeutics was evolved, and the use of charms and incantations yielded in a measure to practical methods. The later Assyrian cuneiform inscriptions (about B. C. 1640) contain references to classified diseases;[112:3] and although healing-spells were still largely in vogue, the employment of various herbs and potions became an important feature in Assyrian Medicine.[113:1]

The therapeutic methods employed by the priests of Finland in early times were chiefly magical. They exorcised the spirits of disease by means of sacred words and healing-spells, which they believed to be of divine origin.[113:2]

Adoration of the hidden forces of nature, and worship of superior beings, gave rise to incantations. It was believed moreover that by the use of appropriate formulas these mysterious powers could be rendered subservient to the will of man. In the popular imagination, even the moon could be made to descend to the earth at the command of an enchantress, by means of an appropriate spell. For, as Virgil sang: Carmina vel possunt coelo deducere lunam.

Among the ancient Aryan peoples, incantations were an important factor in therapeutics, and naturally the use of the same methods persisted among their descendants, after their dispersion and settlement in different parts of the world.

Christianus Pazig, in his "Treatise on Magic Incantations," remarked that the ancient origin of written spells is attested alike by sacred and profane literature. According to tradition, Ham, the son of Noah, inscribed mystic sentences on flinty rocks and metals at the time of the Deluge, in order to preserve them, "being influenced perhaps by the fear that he would not be allowed to take into the Ark a book filled with these vanities." The secret art of preparing incantations is said to have been imparted to others by Mizraim, the son of Ham, and as a result Egypt and Persia were invaded by hordes of magicians, who aspired to dominate universal nature, and to subject to their own wills not only human beings and the lower animals, but even inanimate objects as well. The Roman poet Lucan (born about A. D. 39) wrote in his "Pharsalia,"[114:1] that by the spells of Thessalian witches, there flowed into the obdurate heart a love that entered not there in the course of nature. And to the same authority is accredited the saying that even the world might be made to stand still by means of a suitable incantation; a saying which voiced the popular belief in the miraculous power of words.

There is abundant evidence to show that the phenomena of psycho-therapeutics were known to the ancients, and that Assyrian practitioners effected cures by the agency of suggestion, although they were ignorant of the mode of its operation. The method of treating and curing in a mysterious way has been a widely spread one. It was known in Egypt; in Greece there was the temple of Asklepios or Esculapius; it was prevalent in Rome; it was in vogue during the Middle Ages. There were oracles and shrines and sacred grottos and springs; and their existence and the matters and facts relating to the practices and cures performed at them are quite as well established as are those of Lourdes in France, or of Sainte Anne de Beaupr? in the Province of Quebec. Dr. Pierre Janet is of the opinion that always and everywhere these cures have been effected under the same laws. The maladies that can be cured have always been the same. There are illnesses that could not be vanquished at Asklepios; they are obdurate still at Lourdes. The same things are done to-day that were done in the temples, and under the same conditions and in the same way, and even in the same space of time. This historic similitude shows us that the miraculous cures are all of them subject to the same regular laws. In far-away Japan there exist precisely the same miracle cures as elsewhere. In fact, it seems to have been a matter of independent discovery by investigators all over the world. Dr. Janet is of the opinion that it is not Asklepios that has copied Assyria, or Lourdes that has patterned after the Greeks, but that all have worked independently and have attained to a similar use of the same natural laws.[115:1]

The Anglo-Saxon clergy sanctioned the use of the relics of saints as having curative virtues in nearly all diseases. A hair from a saint's beard, moistened in holy water and taken inwardly, was a favorite remedy for fever.[116:1]

Direct healing power was also ascribed to the tombs of saints, and indeed to anything pertaining to the latter. In the popular view, sacred relics were not only potent to heal, but also brought good fortune. This was true in medieval times, but the early heathen nations had no such beliefs.[116:2] In a recent article in the "Century Magazine," March, 1908, entitled "Christianity and Health," Rev. Samuel McComb, D.D., averred that the relic of a dead superstition may achieve as much, in the cure of physical disorders, as faith in the living God.

The ecclesiastical miracles in the Middle Ages, and the healing wonders in our own time, attested as they are by the highest medical authorities, show what curative power lies in the mere psychological state of trust and confidence. Dr. A. T. Schofield says,[116:3] in explanation of the many seemingly miraculous cures worked at Lourdes and elsewhere, that all the causative changes take place in the unconscious mind, yet the patient is wholly ignorant of anything but the results in the body. Therefore, in such cases, radical cures may be effected instantaneously.

In a lecture on "Temples and Cults in Babylon and Assyria," during his Lowell Institute course at Boston, January 18, 1910, Dr. Morris Jastrow, Jr., spoke of incantation as a popular custom in ancient times.

It is difficult, he said, to draw the line between public and private cults. Divination by means of the liver was an official cult and bore only on public affairs, and there was in its determination a ritual. Astrology, on the contrary, was largely a private affair, and needed but an observation of the heavens, which was done without religious ceremony. When, however, a cult became very popular, the priests were not slow to add its ceremonies to their own.

A most important cult of this nature was incantation. This was against disease and misfortune. Disease was caused by a witch or demon who took possession of the sick one, and cure depended on the ability to get rid of the demon. The elements of fire and water had much to do with the combating of disease, and the two chief deities appealed to were Ea, god of water, and Marduk, god of the sun and fire. In both cases the idea was one of purification. Extended rituals were recited, questions were asked by the priests that demanded almost confessions for their replies.

The physicians of ancient Egypt blended science and superstition in their prescriptions. While fully appreciating the benefit of a stimulus to the patient's imagination, they did not, however, neglect the employment of medicinal remedies.

In a papyrus medical treatise of the sixteenth century B. C., discovered at Thebes in the winter of 1872-73, by the German Egyptologist George Ebers, are to be found numerous incantations and conjurations. Nevertheless the same treatise affords evidence of a careful preparation of complex recipes.[118:1] Some of the prescriptions in this document are considered by Miss Amelia B. Edwards to be of mythological origin, while others appear to have been derived from the medical lore of Syria.[118:2]

Egyptian medical papyri contain both prescriptions for remedies to be used for various ailments, and conjurations for the expulsion of demons, together with petitions for the present intervention of deities.[118:3]

The Chaldean magi also employed many formulas and incantations for repelling evil spirits and for the cure of disease. Specimens of such formulas are to be seen on clay tablets exhumed from the ruins of ancient Nineveh. They consist chiefly in a description of some disease, with the expression of a desire for deliverance from it, and a command enforcing its departure.[119:1] During the preparation of their medicines the ancient Egyptians offered prayers and invocations, of which the following is a specimen:

"May Isis heal me, as she healed Horus, of all the ills inflicted upon him when Set slew his father Osiris. O Isis, thou great Enchantress, free me, deliver me from all evil, bad and horrible things, from the god and goddess of evil, from the god and goddess of sickness, and from the unclean demon who presses upon me, as thou didst loose and free thy son Horus."[119:2]

The Egyptians held the theory that many diseases were due to the anger of Isis, who was also believed by them to have discovered various remedies. Hence the propitiation of this goddess by invocations was a natural expedient.[119:3]

So great was the fondness of the Egyptians for amulets, that they were wont to hang them about the necks of mummies to ward off demons.[119:4] Apropos of this singular custom, we may remark, in passing, that mummy-dust was prescribed by English physicians as late as during the reign of Charles II, to promote longevity. They reasoned that inasmuch as pulverized mummy had lasted a long time, it might, when assimilated by their patients, assist the latter to do likewise.[120:1]

The worship of subterranean deities, representing the hidden forces of nature, is said to have been a chief feature of the religion of the prehistoric Pelasgians inhabiting Greece; and it was believed that if once the particular formula or spell, wherein lay the secret of their power, could be discovered, these deities might be rendered subservient to the will of man.[120:2] Similarly, in many religions of antiquity, the names of deities were invested with great power, and whoever uttered them was "master of the god."[120:3]

Cato the Censor (B. C. 234-149), in his treatise "De Re Rustica," chapter 157, recommended a written charm for the cure of fractures; and Ovid (B. C. 43-A. D. 18), in his "Metamorphoses," wrote these lines: "By means of incantations I break in twain the viper's jaws." In very early times physicians were regarded as under the protection of the gods, and the magical charms employed by them were therefore naturally invested with supernatural curative power. Melampus, a noted mythical leech of Argos, before the Trojan War, was said to have made use of healing-spells in his practice.

Professor H. Bluner, in "The Home Life of the Ancient Greeks," chapter 7, remarks that, in the early historic era, medicine developed especially in two directions in Greece: namely, as practised by a regular medical fraternity; and secondly, "as a kind of religious mystery in the hands of the priests." The latter system was doubtless connected with the worship of Esculapius. But quacks and charlatans were much in evidence, even in that remote epoch. Francis Bacon, in his "Advancement of Learning," chapter 2, says that "the poets were clear-sighted in discerning the credulity of men in often preferring a mountebank, or a cunning woman to a learned physician. Hence they made Esculapius and Circe brother and sister, and both children of Apollo."

The Grecians believed that petitions offered in a foreign tongue were more favorably received than those in the vernacular; and as a reason for this belief it was alleged that the earliest languages, however barbarous and strange to classic ears, contained words and names which were somehow more consonant to nature and hence more pleasing to their deities.[121:1] Especial magical efficacy has always been ascribed to certain Hebrew, Arabian, and Indian words.[121:2]

Alius, who lived at Amida in Mesopotamia in the fifth century, the first Christian physician whose medical writings are extant, repeated biblical verses during the preparation of his medicines, in order to increase their efficacy.[122:1] And until comparatively modern times, the employment of verbal charms, curative spells, and formulas, was believed to enhance the therapeutic virtues of medicines. No remedy, we are told, was administered without mysterious ceremony and incantation.

According to Suidas, a Greek lexicographer, supposed to have lived in the tenth century, the method of curing diseases by the repetition of certain words had been practised ever since the time of the mythological King Minos, of Crete. Indeed, among the peoples of antiquity, the science of therapeutics was largely of a theurgic or supernatural character, and Sibylline verses were in great repute. In this connection it is interesting to note that, according to one authority, the word carminative, a remedy which relieves pain "like a charm," is derived from the Latin carminare, to use incantations.

Words of encouragement and a cheerful mien are good therapeutic agents; and the physician of Plato's day, we are told, sometimes took an orator along with him, in his visits to Grecian households, to persuade his patients to take medicines.[122:2] Such an expedient may have been warranted in those days, but it is of course wholly unnecessary in this age of palatable elixirs and chocolate-coated tablets.

Alexander of Tralles, a Greek physician of the sixth century, recommended a verse of Homer for the cure of colic. In our advanced stage of culture, we should hardly be content with such a carminative, but should rather employ one of the modern aromatic remedies of the pharmacopoeia. In the classic age, however, as well as at later epochs, the use of verbal charms for the cure of disease was forbidden under severe penalties. The case is recorded of a woman of Achaia, who was stoned to death for attempting to cure a fever by the repetition of spells. This was in the fourth century, during the reign of Valentinian.[123:1]

The Greeks invoked Asklepios, the god of Medicine, and his daughters Hygeia, the goddess of Health, and Panacea, the All-Healer, who personified attributes of their father. Apollo, too, under the title of Paen, was worshipped as a health-deity and physician of the gods. He was addressed both as a healer and destroyer; as one who inflicted diseases, but who likewise vouchsafed remedies for their cure. But there appears to have been no incompatibility between the offering of prayers to these heathen deities, and the use of magical spells, formulas and verses. For religion, the healing art, and magic seem to have been inextricably blended in the early days of Greece and Rome, notwithstanding the teachings of Hippocrates, who first strove to liberate medicine from the superstition which enslaved it.

The complex character of therapeutic methods in vogue among the ancient classical peoples, finds a modern parallel in the case of American aborigines. In various tribes the functions of priest, doctor, and wizard are assumed by one and the same person.[124:1] Under the influence of civilization the leech and parson have their distinct professions, and the role of the magician loses much of its importance. In the present advanced stage of culture, many physicians devote themselves to particular branches of their art, and each human organ, when ailing, may invoke assistance from its own special Esculapian.

The Romans of the fourth century, says Edward Gibbon,[124:2] "dreaded the mysterious power of spells and incantations, of potent herbs and mysterious rites, which could extinguish or recall life, inflame the passions of the soul, blast the works of creation, and extort from reluctant demons the secrets of futurity." They held firmly to the belief that this miraculous power was possessed by certain old hags and enchantresses, who lived in poverty and obscurity. The modern popular ideas about witches having compacts with evil spirits, whereby the former are enabled to operate supernaturally, appear to be of very ancient origin, as is evident from the folk-lore of different peoples.

Magical arts, wrote Gibbon, although condemned alike by popular opinion and by the laws of Rome, were continually practised, because they tended to gratify the most imperious passions of men's hearts.

Among pagan nations prayers were somewhat akin to incantations, and were not always regarded as petitions; but their value was supposed to inhere in the power of the uttered words, a power which even the gods were unable to withstand.[125:1] The mystic verses by means of which Athenian physicians anciently invoked supernatural aid, were called carmina, charms,[125:2] their magical nature was incompatible with a purely devotional spirit, and they were therefore incantations rather than prayers. Invocations of deities and magic spells have one point in common; both are appeals to spirits believed to possess supernatural powers. This very kinship may render verbal charms the more obnoxious to devout people, on the same principle which led Lord Bacon to declare superstition to be the more repulsive on account of its similitude to religion, "even as it addeth deformity to an ape to be so like a man." In the prayers offered by the Romans to their deities, the choice of apt phrases was considered to be of greater importance than the mental attitude of the petitioner, because of the prevalent belief in the efficacy of appropriate words per se.

Hence, we are told, when prayers for the welfare of the State were publicly recited by a magistrate, it was customary for a high-priest to dictate suitable expressions, lest an unhappy selection of words provoke divine anger.[126:1] Popular credence attributed to the classic writer Marcus Varro (B. C. 116-28), sometimes called "the most learned of the Romans," the faculty of curing tumors by the direct expression of mental force, namely, by means of words.[126:2]

The Romans believed that the magical power of prayers was enhanced if they were uttered with a loud voice. Hence a saying attributed to Seneca: "So speak to God as though all men heard your prayers." Of great repute among the healing-spells of antiquity was the cabalistic word Abracadabra, which occurs first in a medical treatise entitled "Pr 鎐 epta de Medicina," by the Roman writer Quintus Serenus Samonicus, who flourished in the second century. An inverted triangular figure, formed by writing this word in the manner hereinafter described, was much valued as an antidote against fevers; cloth or parchment being the material originally used for the inscription.

Thou shalt on paper write the spell divine, Abracadabra called, on many a line, Each under each in even order place, But the last letter in each line efface; As by degrees the elements grow few, Still take away, but fix the residue, Till at the last one letter stands alone, And the whole dwindles to a tapering cone. Tie this about the neck with flaxen string, Mighty the good 't will to the patient bring. Its wondrous potency shall guard his bed, And drive disease and death far from his head.[127:1]

Another favorite therapeutic spell, no less venerable than Abracadabra, was the mystical word Abraxas, which was first used by Basilides, a leader of the Egyptian Gnostics in the second century. This word, engraved on an antique precious stone, sometimes accompanied by a magical emblem and meaningless inscription, was commonly used as a medical amulet, and was well adapted to fire the imagination of ignorant patients.

The following curious extract is taken from a rare book published by W. Clowes, serjeant-surgeon to Queen Elizabeth, entitled, "A Proved Practice for all Young Chirurgians," 1588:

It is not long since that a subtile deluder, verie craftely having upon set purpose his brokers or espials abroade, using sundry secret drifts to allure many, as did the syrens by their sweet sonets and melody seduce mariners to make them their pray, so did his brokers or espials deceive many, in proclayming and sounding out his fame abroade from house to house, as those use which crye, "Mistresse, have you any worke for the tincker?" At the lengthe they heard of one that was tormented with a quartaine; then in all post haste this bad man was brought unto the sicke patient by their craftie means, and so forth, without any tariance, he did compound for fifteene pounde to rid him within three fits of his agew, and to make him as whole as a fish of all diseases: so a little before the fit was at hand, he called unto the wife of the patient to bring him an apple of the biggest size, and then with a pinne writte in the rinde of the apple Abracadabra, and such like, and perswaded him to take it presently in the beginning of his fit, for there was (sayeth he) a secret in those words. To be short, the patient, being hungry of his health, followed his counsell, and devoured all and every peece of the apple. So soon as it was receyved, nature left the disease to digest the apple, which was to hard to do; for at length he fell to vomiting, then the core kept such a sturre in his throate, that wheretofore his fever was ill, now much worse, a malo ad pejus, out of the frying-pan into the fire: presently there were physitions sent for unto the sick patient, or else his fifteene pound had been gone, with a more pretious jewell: but this lewde fellow is better knowne at Newgate than I will heere declare.[128:1]

Certain mystic sentences of barbaric origin, mostly unintelligible, and known as "Ephesian Letters," engraved upon the famous statue of Diana at Ephesus, were popular among the Greeks as charms wherewith to drive away diseases, to render the wearer invincible in battle, or to purify demon-infested places. Their invention was attributed to the fabulous Dactyls of Phrygia, and they appear to have been held in equally great esteem, whether pronounced orally as incantations, or inscribed upon strips of parchment and worn as amulets.

In ancient Hibernia, the former western limit of the known world, the Druids, in their medical treatment, relied much upon magic rites and incantations.[129:1] And the early Irish physicians, who belonged to the Druid priesthood, were devoted to mystical medicine, although they also prescribed various herbs with whose therapeutic use they were familiar.[129:2] In Ireland according to Lady Wilde,[129:3] invocations were formerly in the names of the Phenician god Baal, and of the Syrian goddess Ashtoreth, representing the sun and moon respectively. . . . After the establishment of Christianity, formulas of invocation were usually in the names of Christ or the Holy Trinity, and those of Mary, Peter, and numerous saints were also used. In Brand's "Popular Antiquities,"[129:4] we find a long list of the names of saints who were invoked for the cure of particular ailments; and the same authority quotes from a work entitled "The Irish Hubbub," by Barnaby Rich, 1619, these lines: "There is no disease, no sicknesse, no greefe, either amongst men or beasts, that hath not his physician among the saints."

The devotion of the Teutonic tribes to magical medicine is not surprising to any one versed in the mythological lore of Scandinavia, which is replete with sorcery. And throughout the Middle Ages, although medical practice was largely in the hands of Christian priests and monks, yet sorcerers and charlatans continued to employ old pagan usages and magical remedies. The German physicians of the Carlovingian era pretended to cure ailments by whispering in the patient's ear, as well as by the use of enchanted herbs. They inherited ceremonial formulas from the practitioners of an earlier age, for the treatment of ophthalmic diseases; and in addition to such spells, they made use of various gestures, and were wont to thrice touch the affected eyes.[130:1]

In Grimm's "Teutonic Mythology"[130:2] is to be found an old German spell against gout, as follows: "God, the Lord went over the land; there met him 70 sorts of gouts and goutesses. Then spake the Lord: 'Ye 70 gouts and goutesses, whither would ye?' Then spake the 70 gouts and goutesses: 'We go over the land and take from men their health and limbs.' Then spake the Lord: 'Ye shall go to an elder-bush and break off all his boughs, and leave with [such an one, naming the patient] his straight limbs.'"

Many old German healing-spells contain the names of our Lord and of the Virgin, which probably superseded those of pagan deities and sacred mythological personages, the formulas remaining otherwise the same. Such spells are akin to pious invocations or actual prayers. Others exhibit a blending of devotion and credulity, and appear to have degenerated into mere verbal forms.

According to a tradition of the North, while Wodan and Baldur were once on a hunting excursion, the latter's horse dislocated a leg; whereupon Wodan reset the bones by means of a verbal charm. And the mere narration of this prehistoric magical cure is in repute in Shetland as a remedy for lameness in horses at the present day.

A remarkable cure for intermittent fever, in a marshy district of Lincolnshire, is described in "Folk-Lore," June, 1898 (page 186). An old woman, whose grandson had a bad attack of the fever, fastened upon the foot-board of his bed three horse-shoes, with a hammer laid cross-wise upon them. With the hammer the old crone gave each shoe a smart tap, repeating each time this spell: "Father, Son, and Holy Ghost, nail the Devil to this post, one for God and one for Wod and one for Lok. . . . Yon's a sure charm," said she, "that will hold the Old One as fast as t' church tower, when next he comes to shake un." The chronicler of this curious incantation calls attention to the association of the name of God with two heathen personages: Wodan, the chief ruler, and Loki, the spirit of evil, in the mythology of the North.

The early Saxons in England knew little of scientific medicine, and relied on indigenous herbs. They were much addicted to the use of wizard spells, a term which originated with them; and were too ignorant to adopt the skilled methods of the practitioners of Greece and Italy.

The invention of some especially forceful words for exorcising fiends and illnesses was ascribed to Robert Grosseteste (about 1175-1253), Bishop of Lincoln; and the fact that a learned prelate should devote attention to the subject is strong testimony to its importance in medieval times. There is indeed abundant evidence that throughout that period verbal charms were very commonly worn, whether devotional sentences, prayer formulas written on vellum, or mystic letters, words, and symbols inscribed on parchment.[132:1] For many centuries medical practice consisted largely of prayers and incantations, the employment of charms and talismans, and the performance of superstitious rites. Until the seventeenth century these methods were more or less in vogue. Thus, a verse from the Lamentations of Jeremiah was thought to be a specific for rheumatism.[133:1]

The Atharva-Veda, one of the ancient Vedas, or religious books of the Hindus, contains hundreds of healing-spells, as well as formulas to secure prosperity, in expiation of sin, and as safeguards against robbers and wild beasts. They are repeated either by the person expecting assistance therefrom, or by a magician for his benefit. Of the therapeutic verses brief examples are here given:

(A charm against fever.) "O Takman (fever), along with thy brother balasa, along with thy sister cough, along with thy cousin paman, go to yonder foreign folk!"

(A charm against cough.) "As a well-sharpened arrow swiftly to a distance flies, thus do thou, O Cough, fly along the expanse of the earth!"

(A charm against the demons of disease.) "O amulet of ten kinds of wood, release this man from the demon and the fit which has seized upon his joints!"

While reciting the above formula, a talisman consisting of splinters from ten kinds of wood is fastened upon the patient, and ten of his friends rub him down.[133:2]

The following translation of an old Scottish incantation against disease is taken from a collection of charms, chiefly of the Outer Hebrides Islands, and included by Alexander Carmichael in his "Carmina Gaelica," Edinburgh, 1900.

Peter and James and John, The Three of sweetest virtues in glory, Who arose to make the charm, Before the great gate of the City, By the right knee of God the Son, Against the keen-eyed men, Against the peering-eyed women, Against the slim, slender, fairy darts, Against the swift arrows of fairies. Two made to thee the withered eye, Man and woman in venom and envy, Three whom I will set against them. Father, Son, and Spirit Holy. Four-and-twenty diseases in the constitution of man and beast. God scrape them, God search them, God cleanse them, From out thy blood, from out thy flesh, From out thy fragrant bones, From this day, and each day that comes, Till thy day on earth be done.

FOOTNOTES:

[111:1] A. J. L. Jourdan, Histoire de la Medecine, tome ii, p. 139.

[112:1] Encyclopedia Britannica, art. "Babylonia."

[112:2] Francis Lenormant, Chaldean Magic, p. 45.

[112:3] Hermann Peters, Pictorial History of Pharmacy.

[113:1] A. Laurent, La Magie et le Divination chez les Chaldeo-Assyriens, p. 33.

[113:2] Francis Lenormant, Chaldean Magic, p. 244.

[114:1] Book vi, 452.

[115:1] Lowell Institute Lecture; Boston, November, 1906.

[116:1] John Thrupp, The Anglo-Saxon Home, p. 277.

[116:2] Jacob Grimm, Teutonic Mythology, p. 1177.

[116:3] The Unconscious Mind, pp. 348-349.

[118:1] Journal of Science, vol. xiii, p. 101; 1876.

[118:2] Pharaohs, Fellahs, and Explorers, p. 219.

[118:3] Alfred Wiedmann, Religion of the Ancient Egyptians, p. 272.

[119:1] Francis Lenormant, Chaldean Magic, p. 12.

[119:2] Johann Hermann Baas, The History of Medicine, tr. by H. E. Henderson, p. 23.

[119:3] R. Dunglison, History of Medicine, p. 23.

[119:4] Boston Transcript, March 4, 1900.

[120:1] A. Lang, Myth, Ritual, and Religion, vol. i, p. 96.

[120:2] Larousse, Grand Dictionnaire, art. "Incantation."

[120:3] T. Witton Davies, Magic, Divination, and Demonology, p. 62.

[121:1] John Potter, Antiquities of Greece, vol. ii, p. 244.

[121:2] Georg Conrad Horst, Zauber-Bibliothek, vol. iii, p. 62.

[122:1] Alfred C. Garratt, M.D., Myths in Medicine, p. 47; Dublin University Magazine, Feb., 1874, p. 221.

[122:2] J. P. Mahaffy, Greek Antiquities, p. 71.

[123:1] J. B. Thiers, Trait?des Superstitions, p. 420.

[124:1] Herbert Spencer, Principles of Sociology, vol. iii, p. 37.

[124:2] The History of the Decline and Fall of the Roman Empire.

[125:1] M'Clintock and Strong, Biblical Cyclopedia, art. "Incantations."

[125:2] Kurt Sprengel, Histoire de la Medecine, tome i, p. 123.

[126:1] Rodolfo Lanciani, A Manual of Roman Antiquities, p. 357.

[126:2] Frank Granger, The Worship of the Romans, p. 227.

[127:1] C. W. King, The Gnostics and their Remains, p. 316.

[128:1] Archeologia, vol. xxx, pp. 427-28; 1884.

[129:1] Brand, Popular Antiquities, vol. iii, p. 269.

[129:2] Ancient Legends, Mystic Charms, and Superstitions of Ireland, vol. ii, p. 74.

[129:3] Ancient Cures, Charms, and Usages of Ireland, p. 9.

[129:4] Vol. i, pp. 356 seq.

[130:1] George F. Fort, Medical Economy during the Middle Ages, p. 296.

[130:2] Vol. iv, p. 1698.

[132:1] George F. Fort, Medical Economy, p. 296.

[133:1] Robley Dunglison, History of Medicine, p. 18.

[133:2] The Sacred Books of the East, edited by F. Max Muller, vol. xlii, p. 2.

CHAPTER XI

MEDICINAL RUNIC INSCRIPTIONS

The discovery of the script of the ancient Germans, supposed to be of Egyptian or Phenician origin, was attributed to Wodan, who was regarded as the chief expert in magical writing. The so-called noxious runes were thought to bring evil upon enemies; the helpful ones averted misfortune, while the medicinal runes were credited with healing properties.[135:1] These ancient characters formed the earliest alphabets among the Germanic peoples, and are found throughout Scandinavia, as well as in Great Britain, France, and Spain, engraved upon monuments, stones, coins, and domestic utensils. The Gothic word runa meant originally a secret magical character, and was used to signify a mysterious speech, song, or writing. The reputed inherent therapeutic qualities of medicinal runes were potent psychic factors, through the subconscious mind, in healing disease.

The Anglo-Saxons made use of runic inscriptions, not only as curatives, but also to banish melancholy and evil thoughts. After their conversion to Christianity, biblical texts were substituted for the runes, and the art of composing the former was studied with as much care as had been devoted to the heathen charms.[136:1] The term rune became a synonym for knowledge and wisdom; an oracular, proverbial expression.[136:2] The traditional belief of the Anglo-Saxons in the efficacy of healing runes persisted in the fourteenth century. When foreign medical practitioners settled in England at that period, the cures wrought by them were attributed to the superior virtues of the charms employed, rather than to their professional skill.[136:3]

The ancient Saxons, before their arrival in Britain, were wont to go forth into battle, having engraven upon their spears certain runic characters, which were valued as protective charms, and served to inspire confidence on the part of the warriors. These magic inscriptions were believed to have been either invented or improved by Wodan, who taught the art of putting them into rhyme, and engraving them upon tables of stone.[136:4] In William Camden's "Britannia,"[136:5] are described divers medicinal inscriptions, found in Cumberland. These were used as spells among the borderers even as late as the close of the eighteenth century. A book of such charms, of that era, taken from the pocket of a moss-trooper or bog-trotter, contained among other things a recipe for the cure of intermittent fever by certain barbarous characts.

In Paul B. du Chaillu's work, "The Viking Age" (London, 1889), mention is made of the ancient northern custom of employing runes as medical charms.

One Egil went on a journey to Vermaland, and on the way he came to the house of a farmer named Thorfinn, whose daughter, Helga, had long been ill of a wasting sickness. "Has anything been tried for her illness?" asked Egil. "Runes have been traced by the son of a farmer in the neighborhood," said Thorfinn.

Then Egil examined the bed, and found a piece of whalebone with runes on it. He read them, cut them off, and scraped the chips into the fire. He also burned the whalebone, and had Helga's clothes carried into the open air. Then Egil sang:

As man shall not trace runes, except he can read them well, it is thus with many a man, that the dark letters bewilder him. I saw on the cut whalebone ten hidden letters carved, that have caused the woman a very long sorrow.

Egil traced runes and placed them under Helga's pillow. It seemed to her as if she awoke from a sleep, and she said that she was then healed.[138:1]

The ancient northern peoples wore protective and defensive amulets, which were fastened around the arm, waist, or neck. These amulets were styled ligamenta, ligature or phylacteria, by the writers of the early Middle Ages. They were usually fashioned as gold, silver, or glass pendants. Cipher-writing and runes were commonly inscribed upon them, often for healing, but contrariwise, to bewitch and injure.[138:2]

Among the peoples of Western Europe, ancient magical healing formulas, relics of previous ages, were employed in medieval times by rural charlatans, who professed to cure ophthalmic disorders by the recitation of ritualistic phrases, together with suitable gestures of the arms and fingers over the affected eyes. Dislocations were said to have been promptly reduced by means of runic enchantments, which were doubtless supplemented by mechanical treatment; while fractured bones of man or beast were alleged to unite readily under the influence of Odinic charms. Wherever the Teutonic races were found, a knowledge of runic remedies appears to have prevailed.[138:3]

FOOTNOTES:

[135:1] M. Mallet, Northern Antiquities, p. 226.

[136:1] John Thrupp, The Anglo-Saxon Home.

[136:2] Nelson's Encyclopedia.

[136:3] H. D. Traill, Social England, vol. ii, p. 110.

[136:4] Joseph Strutt, Manners of the English, vol. i, p. 17.

[136:5] Vol. iii, p. 455.

[138:1] The Egil's Saga, chap. 72.

[138:2] Jacob Grimm, Teutonic Mythology, pp. 1173-1174.

[138:3] George F. Fort, Medical Economy in the Middle Ages.

CHAPTER XII

METALLO-THERAPY

Metallo-therapy has been defined as a mode of treating various affections, chiefly those of a nervous character, by the external application of metals. It was recommended by Galen and other medical writers, but they attributed its curative powers to the magical inscriptions which the metals bore.

Mesmer experimented with magnets extensively, but soon abandoned their use, as he found that he could obtain equally good results without them.

The so-called "metallic tractors" originated with Dr. Elisha Perkins (1740-1799), a practising physician of Norwich, Connecticut, and consisted of two rods, one of brass, and the other of steel. In cases of rheumatism and various neuroses, the affected portions of the body were lightly stroked by means of the tractors, and many remarkable cures were reported. The new therapeutic method was endorsed by many reputable practitioners, both in the United States and Europe, and its fame spread like wild-fire.

It was soon discovered, however, that wooden tractors were fully as efficacious as the metallic ones, and that the many vaunted cures were psychic. Thus Perkins's tractors afford a striking example of the curative force of suggestion.

Thereby (wrote John Haygarth, M.D., Fellow of the Royal Medical Society of Edinburgh, in a brief treatise on the Imagination, published in the year 1800) is to be learned an important lesson in Medicine, namely, the wonderful and powerful influence of the passions of the mind, upon the state and disorders of the body. This fact, he continued, was too often overlooked in Practice, where sole dependence was placed upon material remedies, without utilizing mental influence. To the latter, this sagacious physician, writing more than a century ago, was shrewd enough to ascribe the marvellous cures attributed to the remedies of quacks, whose magnificent and unqualified promises inspire weak minds with confidence.

In one of his Lowell Institute lectures, at Boston, November 14, 1906, Dr. Pierre Janet described the development of metallo-therapy in France between the years 1860 and 1880. Metallic discs were applied to the patient's body. These discs were of different kinds, sometimes being composed of two or more metals. In some cases a magnet was used. Different subjects, it was found, did not manifest sensitiveness to the same metals, some being cured by iron, others by copper, while the greatest number were susceptible to gold. Many interesting facts relating to these cures were noted, such as periods of transition and oscillation in the maladies, and most curious of all, a kind of transference. For example, should a paralysis or a contraction seat itself on the right side, the application of the discs would effect a cure, but the malady would often return to the opposite side. And there were other curious phenomena. A modification of sensation was invariably observed.

Under the influence of the metal disc, the shin and muscles, which before were numb, regained their normal states, and the return of sensation preceded the cure, and was an indispensable condition. One can obtain exactly the same results with discs composed of inert substances. An old-fashioned letter-wafer, for instance, applied to the hand, has produced similar effects. According to Dr. Janet, these phenomena are wholly due to psychic agencies, partly akin to suggestion and partly different. They depend upon the mechanism of attention. This faculty, when directed upon any organ, will bring into prominence sensations not ordinarily felt.

Consciousness is limited, in that it does not always take cognizance of all the existing sensations. This explains the phenomenon of transference, in that the suppression of those sensations which were prominent brings to the surface others which were not before recognized by the consciousness.

As a result of the introduction of metallo-therapy in the hospitals of Paris, an enormous number of hysterical patients applied for treatment, influenced partly, no doubt, by the love of notoriety.

CHAPTER XIII

ANIMAL MAGNETISM

Although curative attributes were ascribed to the magnet in ancient times, and the same belief prevailed in the Middle Ages, the noted charlatan Paracelsus (1493-1541) was the first to propound the theory of the existence of magnetic properties in the human body. During the seventeenth century several persons in Great Britain claimed the ability to cure diseases by stroking with the hand, and of these the most notable was the celebrated Irish empiric, Valentine Greatrakes (1628-1700).

It was asserted, moreover, by certain practitioners, that by magnetizing a sword it could be made to cure any wound which the sword had inflicted. And about the year 1625, Dr. Robert Fludd, an English physician of learning and repute, introduced the famous "weapon-salve," which became immensely popular. Its ingredients consisted of moss growing on the head of a thief who had been hanged, mummy dust, human blood, suet, linseed oil, and Armenian bole, a species of clay. All these were mixed thoroughly in a mortar. The sword, after being dipped in the blood from the wound, was carefully anointed with the precious mixture, and laid by in a cool place. Then the wound was cared for according to the most approved surgical methods, with thorough cleansing and bandaging.

The successful results naturally attending this treatment were attributed by the ignobile vulgus to the wonderful ointment. There were sceptics who denied its efficacy, but the new remedy appealed to the popular imagination. However, a certain Pastor Foster issued a pamphlet entitled "A Spunge to wipe away the Weapon-Salve," which latter the writer affirmed to be an invention of the Devil, who gave it to Paracelsus, by whom it was bequeathed to the eminent Italian physician, Giambattista della Porta, and finally was acquired by Doctor Fludd. In reply to this attack, the latter published a vigorous refutation, under the following caption: "The Squeezing of Parson

Foster's Spunge, wherein the Spunge-bearer's immodest carriage and behaviour towards his brethren, is Detected; the Bitter Flames of his slanderous reports are, by the sharp Vinegar of Truth, Corrected and quite Extinguished, and lastly, the virtuous validity of his Spunge in wiping away the Weapon-Salve, is crushed out and clean abolished."

In commenting on certain superstitious methods in surgery, which were in vogue in the sixteenth century, the noted chemist and physician, Andrew Libavius, a native of Halle, in Saxony, remarked that while wounds are healed by nature, pretended magical remedies may be of use by directing the natural forces to the spot, through the imagination.

Another favorite remedy, somewhat akin to the weapon-salve, was the so-called "sympathetic powder," which was said to consist of sulphate of copper prepared with mysterious ceremonies.

According to popular report, the recipe was brought from the East by a Carmelite friar, and was introduced in England by Sir Kenelm Digby, a noted chemist and philosopher of the seventeenth century, who was also a Gentleman of the Bedchamber of Charles I. He published a volume on the healing of wounds by means of this preparation. Portions of the patient's bloodstained apparel were immersed in a solution of the sympathetic powder, the wound meantime being cleansed and bandaged. A strictly enforced regimen also formed part of the treatment.

As may readily be inferred, this wonderful powder, like the weapon-salve, was equally efficacious, whether used at a distance from the patient, or near by.

But it has ever been true, that the positive and reiterated assertions of a charlatan will usually avail to delude not only the wonder-loving public, but even persons of intellect and distinction. The secret of the sympathetic powder became known to Dr. Theodore Turquet de Mayerne (at one time the chief physician of James I), who is said to have derived considerable profit from the sale of this once famous nostrum.[146:1]

The system of therapeutics known as Mesmerism, originated by Friedrich Anton Mesmer (1733-1815), a German physician, affords a notable example of the influence of the mind upon the body through the imagination. In its essential principles, it does not materially differ from the ancient method of healing by laying-on of hands. As a young man Mesmer became interested in astrology, believing that the stars exert, according to their relative position at certain times, a direct influence upon human beings. He at first identified this supposed force with electricity, and afterwards with magnetism. Later he claimed to be endowed with a mysterious power available for the cure of various diseases. Removing to Paris in 1778, Mesmer at once began to demonstrate his theories, maintaining that he was able to exercise a therapeutic effect upon his patients, by virtue of a magnetic fluid proceeding from him, or simply by the domination of his will over that of the patient.

He asserted that the magnetic fluid is the medium of a mutual influence between the stars, the earth, and human beings. By insinuating itself into the substance of the nerves of the human body, it affects them at once, being moreover capable of communication from one body to other bodies, animate or inanimate. It perfects the action of medicines, and heals affections of the nerves. In animal magnetism nature presents a universal method of benefiting mankind. Such, at least, was the declaration of Mesmer.[147:1]

With a view to influencing the imaginations of his patients, this shrewd practitioner caused his consulting apartments in Paris to be dimly lighted and surrounded by mirrors. Strains of soft music were heard, subtle odors pervaded the air, and the patients were seated around a circular oaken trough or baquet, in which were disposed a row of bottles containing so-called electrical fluid. A complicated system of wires connected the mouths of the bottles with handles, which were grasped by the patients. After the latter had waited for a while in expectant silence, Mesmer would appear, wearing a coat of lilac silk, and carrying a magician's wand, which he manipulated in a graceful and mysterious manner. Then, discarding the wand, he passed his hands over the bodies of the patients for a considerable time, "until the magnetized person was saturated with the healing fluid."

So great was the interest aroused by Mesmer's methods and the many seemingly marvellous cures resulting therefrom, that the Royal Society of Paris appointed a commission, which included Benjamin Franklin, to investigate the subject. The members of this commission reported that those patients who were not aware of the fact that they were being magnetized experienced no effects from the treatment. Those who were told that they were being magnetized experienced symptoms, although the magnetizer was not near them. Imagination, apart from magnetism, produced marked effects, while magnetism, without imagination, produced nothing. The benefits resulting from Mesmer's treatment were due, according to the commission's report, to three factors, namely: (1) actual contact; (2) the excitement of the imagination; and (3) "the mechanical imitation which impels us to repeat that which strikes our senses."

The ability to cure disease without the use of medicines or surgical appliances has been claimed by alleged healers in all ages. When such cures were effected, they were attributed to a special gift with which the healer was divinely endowed, and this gift was bestowed, in rare instances, upon individuals who were distinguished by especial sanctity. Mesmer did not claim this quality, and yet he performed cures which were as notable as those of any saint or inspired healer of earlier times. He believed that through animal magnetism a direct physical effect was exerted upon the human body. And this effect he held to be due to the virtues of a subtle fluid.

Frank Podmore, in "Mesmerism and Christian Science" (1909), expresses the belief that Mesmer obtained many of his ideas from his contemporary, Gassner. For even if he did not actually meet the latter, Mesmer must have known him by reputation and doubtless was familiar with his methods of healing. Gassner was a believer in the demoniac theory of disease, and sought to expel the evil spirit by chasing it from one part of the body to another, finally driving it out by word of command, from the fingers or toes. Similar procedures were characteristic of Mesmer's earlier methods, but were not retained by his successors.

One of Mesmer's most prominent followers was Armand Marc Jacques de Chastenet, Marquis de Puysur, born of noble ancestry at Paris, March 1, 1751. He entered early upon a military career, and attained by successive promotions the rank of colonel in the Royal Artillery in 1778. Serving with distinction at the siege of Gibraltar during the Spanish campaign, he was appointed field-marshal in 1789, and lieutenant-general in 1814. Meanwhile he had become greatly interested in the subject of animal magnetism, having been at one time a pupil of Mesmer, whom he had assisted at the latter's seances. Retiring to his chateau at Buzancy, Department of Aisne, in northern

France, he devoted himself to the study of the phenomena of mesmerism, and to practical experimentation of its therapeutic value in the open air, beneath the dense foliage of the forests, after the style of the ancient Druids. Puysur introduced new methods of magnetizing, and demonstrated that many of the resultant phenomena could be made to appear by gentle manipulation, and without the mysterious appliances and violent procedures of Mesmer. Mindful of the latter's assertion that wood could be magnetized, he decided to experiment upon a large elm tree which grew upon the village green. As a result, streams of magnetic fluids were alleged to pass from its branches by means of cords twisted around the bodies of patients, who sat in a circle about the tree, with thumbs interlocked, in order to afford a direct passage for the healing influence.

In his work entitled "Memoires pour servir l'histoire et l'establissement du Magnisme Animal" (London, 1786), Puysur affirmed his belief in the ancient doctrine of the existence of a universal fluid, vivifying all nature, and always in motion. This doctrine he maintained to be an ancient truth, the rejection whereof was due to ignorance. He continued his researches and practice until his death at Buzancy, August 1, 1825.

The magnetic fluid, according to some authorities, may be reflected like light or propagated like sound, and increased, opposed, accumulated, and transmitted to another object. Moreover this principle, which is akin to a sixth sense, artificially acquired, may be employed for the cure of nervous affections, by provoking and directing salutary crises, thus bringing the healing art to perfection.

Mesmerism clearly appears to be no more than an antecedent of hypnotism; few, if any, of the distinctive features of the modern science appearing in an appreciated form in its practices. Mesmer had little experience and no appreciation of the hypnotic state, or of the phenomena of suggestion; he constantly elaborated his physical manipulations, denied the imagination any place in his effects, and regarded the crisis as the distinctive and essential factor in his cures; and when confronted with subjects in hypnotic state, pronounced the production of this state as foolish and regarded it as a subordinate phase of the magnetic crisis.[151:1]

Thomson Jay Hudson, in his volume, "The Law of Mental Medicine," affirms that the therapeutic successes of the ancient method of laying-on of hands, the King's touch, metallic tractors, and mesmerism are fully explained by the doctrine of suggestion, the mental energy of the healer being transmitted as a therapeutic impulse from his subjective mind through the medium of the nerves to the affected cells of the patient's body, connection being established by so-called cellular rapport, that is, "by bringing into physical contact the nerve-terminals of the two personalities."

The distinguished psychologist, James Braid, said that whoever supposes that the power of imagination is merely a mental emotion, which may vary to any extent, without corresponding changes in the physical functions, labors under a mighty mistake. Suggestions by others of the ideas of health, vigor, and hope, are influential with many people for restoring health and energy both of mind and body. Having then such an effective power to work with, the great desideratum has been to find the best means for regulating and controlling it, so as to render it subservient to our will for relieving and curing diseases. The modes devised, both by mesmerists and hypnotists, for these ends, are a real, solid, and important addition to practical therapeutics.[152:1]

The importance of suggestive healing methods can hardly be overestimated, and has been emphasized by many writers. Notable among recent publications on the subject are Dr. T. J. Hudson's work, entitled "The Law of Psychic Phenomena," and Dr. A. T. Schofield's "Unconscious Mind." Dr. Pierre Janet, in one of his Lowell Institute lectures, in Boston, November 3, 1906, remarked that

Before the time of Mesmer the sleep produced by magnetizers was really the cause of numberless cures. Hypnotism, which has replaced it little by little since 1840, and has been more rapidly developed since 1878, differs from its ancestor more in the interpretation of the phenomena than in the practices themselves. It has naturally had the same therapeutic applications, and its methods are probably legitimate. Hypnotic sleep has had many helpful influences. It is really a change in the equilibrium of the brain and mental faculties and produces great modifications in the memory and in sensibility. Life is indeed a long series of habits to which we are accustomed; hypnotism changes these habits which in a normal condition we do not try to modify, and on awakening, all memory of the change is gone, although its effects may remain.

Now oftentimes the nervous system becomes fixed in certain disagreeable or dangerous habits, and the upsetting of these, the uplifting of the mind from the rut, is of great service. In the sleep of hypnotism speech, action, methods of thought, all are changed, there is a cerebral rest, and beneficial results often follow.

From the period following Braid's contributions up to the foundation of modern hypnotism, . . . the history of the subject may be briefly told. The field is occupied largely by propagandists of one or another of the extravagant forms of animal magnetism . . . by traveling mesmerists, by sensationally advertised subjects, and by a small and unorganized number of scientific men, attempting to stem the tide of mysticism and error with which the others were deluging the public. The recognition of hypnotism as an altered physiological and psychological condition, after repeated demonstrations, at last gained the day, securing for the phenomena a place in the accepted body of scientific doctrines.[153:1]

Professor Bernheim says that the hypnotic condition and the phenomena associated therewith are purely subjective, and originate in the nervous system of the patient.

The fixation of a brilliant object, so that the muscle which holds up the upper eyelid becomes fatigued, and the concentration of the attention on a single idea, bring about the sleep. The subjects can even bring about this condition in themselves, by their own tension of mind, without being submitted to any influence from without. In this state the imagination becomes so lively that every idea spontaneously developed or suggested, by a person to whom the subject gives this peculiar attention and confidence, has the value of an actual representation to him.[154:1]

It has been well said that if Mesmer's methods served only to demonstrate the curative power of the imagination, they have been of some benefit to humanity.

The consideration of hypnotic cures does not appertain to our theme. Far from these being primitive methods, they represent what is most modern and advanced in psycho-therapeutics.

FOOTNOTES:

[146:1] Francis J. Shepherd, M.D., Medical Quacks and Quackery.

[147:1] F. A. Mesmer, Moire sur la Duverte du Magnisme Animal; Paris, 1779.

[151:1] The Cosmopolitan, vol. xx, p. 363.

[152:1] Braid, Neurypnology, p. 338.

[153:1] The Cosmopolitan, February, 1896.

[154:1] H. Bernheim, M.D., Suggestive Therapeutics, p. 111.

CHAPTER XIV

ANCIENT MEDICAL PRESCRIPTIONS

From early times it was a universal custom to place at the beginning of a medical prescription certain religious verses or superstitious characters, which formed the invocation, or prayer to a favorite deity.[155:1] Angelic beings were frequently appealed to, and among these the Archangel Raphael was thought to be omnipotent for the cure of disease. John Aubrey, in his "Miscellanies," relates that a certain physician, Dr. Richard Nepier, a person of great piety, whose knees were horny with much praying, was wont to ask professional advice of this archangel, and that his prescriptions began with the abbreviation "R. Ris." for Responsum Raph, Raphael's answer. The name of Raphael was often seen on amulets and talismans. But our information regarding this angel is derived chiefly from the Book of Tobit, where Raphael is represented as the guide and counsellor of the young Tobias. In one of the later Midrashim, Raphael appears as the angel commissioned to put down the evil spirits that vexed the sons of Noah with plagues and sicknesses after the Flood, and he it was who taught men the use of "simples," and furnished materials for the "Book of Noah," the earliest treatise on materia medica.[156:1]

A recent writer affirms that [Rx] is the emblem of the sun-god Ra, and signifies "In the name of Ra," or "Ra, God of Life and Health, inspire me."[156:2] This deity was regarded as the Supreme Being, not only by the Egyptians, but by other heathen people of antiquity, because the sun was the greatest and most brilliant of the planets.

In Egyptian hieroglyphics[156:3] Ra was represented as a hawk-headed man, holding in one hand the symbol of life, and in the other the royal sceptre.

The medical symbol [Rx], still in use at the present day, owes its origin, however, neither to the angel Raphael nor to the god Ra. It is the ancient sign of Jupiter. This sign, which also symbolized the metal tin, had many modifications, some of which were as follows: [Symbol: Jupiter], [Symbol: Jupiter], [Symbol: Jupiter].

These were gradually replaced by the letter R, or its astrological modification [Rx], which was equivalent to Recipe, Jupiter,--Take, O Jupiter! We are told that the astrological signs were thus brought into use during Nero's reign, and that the practice of Medicine was then and afterwards regulated by the government. It is not improbable that Christian physicians were obliged to follow the example of their heathen professional brethren in prefixing to their prescriptions invocations to Jupiter.[157:1]

Johann Michael Moscherosch (1600-1669), a learned German writer, offered a unique explanation of the meaning of the medical symbol [Rx], which he maintained to be equivalent to Rec, an abbreviation for per decem. And he explained the significance of the latter as being that one prescription out of ten might be expected to prove beneficial to the patient. It is certain, wrote Dr. Otto A. Wall, in his volume, "The Prescription," that pharmacies for the dispensing of medicines on physicians' prescriptions were already in existence at the ancient Spanish city of Cordova, and at other large municipalities under the control of the Arabs, previous to the twelfth century. And as early as 1233, pharmacy laws had already been passed in the Two Sicilies. By that time, it appears probable that medical prescriptions were no longer mere superstitious formulas, but that they contained directions for compounding material remedies having more or less medicinal virtues.

Modern medical prescriptions may be classed as lineal descendants of the healing-spells of former ages. In the most ancient known pharmacopoeia, a papyrus discovered about the year 1858 in the Necropolis at Thebes, and believed to date from the sixteenth century B. C., no invocations or symbols are found, nor were the latter generally employed as prefixes to medical formulas prior to the first century A. D.; when their use appears to have originated among the Greeks and Romans, and the custom has continued until the present day. At the time of the alchemists, in the sixteenth century, "the influence of the Church on the minds of men, or perhaps the fear of the Inquisition, led physicians to adopt an invocation to the Christian God; just as they abbreviated a prayer to crossing themselves with their fingers over their foreheads and breasts, so they contracted the invocation to the sign of the cross as a superscription."[158:1]

Thus instead of the sign [Rx] some physicians began their prescriptions with the Greek letters +Alpha.+ +Omega.+; or the letters J. D. for Juvante Deo, C. D. for Cum Deo, or N. D. for Nomine Dei.

Dr. Rodney H. True, lecturer on botany at Harvard College, in a paper on Folk Materia Medica, read at a meeting of the Boston branch of the American Folk-Lore Society, February 19, 1901, gave a list of therapeutic agents, mostly of animal origin, forming the stock in trade of a European druggist some two hundred years ago. This list includes the fats, gall, blood, marrow from bones, teeth, livers, and lungs of various animals, birds, and reptiles; also bees, crabs, and toads, incinerated after drying; amber, shells, coral, claws, and horns; hair from deer and cats; ram's wool, partridge feathers, ants, lizards, leeches, earth-worms, pearl, musk, and honey; eyes of the wolf, pickerel, and crab; eggs of the hen and ostrich, cuttlefish bone, dried serpents, and the hoofs of animals.

With the development of materia medica in Europe, the use of animal drugs diminished; but during the last decade of the nineteenth century, extracts of animal organs were manufactured on a large scale, and found a ready market. Thus some of the articles mentioned are reckoned among remedial agents to-day, but most of them doubtless owed their virtues to mental action. Wolf's eyes in former times and bread pills nowadays may be cited as typical remedies, acting through the patient's imagination and possessing no intrinsic curative properties, yet nevertheless valuable articles of the pharmacopoeia from the standpoint of suggestive therapeutics. In a list of Japanese quack medicines, of the present time, we find mention of "Spirit-cheering" pills.[159:1]

In "A Booke of Physicke and Chirurgery, with divers other things necessary to be knowne, collected out of sundry olde written bookes, and broughte into one order. Written in the year of our Lorde God 1610," among many curious prescriptions we find the following: "A good oyntment against the vanityes of the heade. Take the juice of worm woode and salte, honye, waxe and incens, and boyle them together over the fire, and therewith anoynte the sick heade and temples." The volume referred to was the property of Mr. William Pickering, an apparitor of the Consistory Court at Durham, England.

A commentator on the above prescription observed that few coxcombs, dandies, and heads filled with bitter conceits, would like to be anointed with this cure of self-sufficiency. The wax might make the plaster stick, but it might be feared that the honey and the incense would neutralize the good effects to be expected from the wormwood and salt. If, however, the phrase "vanityes of the head" be interpreted to mean a dearth of ideas, we may assume that the above prescription was intended as a stimulus to the imagination, and as such it might well have a therapeutic value.

Dr. William Salmon, a London practitioner, published in the year 1693 "A Short Manual of Physick, designed for the general use of Her Majestie's subjects, accommodated to mean capacities, in order to the Restauration of their Healths."

In this little volume we find a prescription for "an Elixer Universall, not particular for any distemper," as follows:

[Rx] Rex Metallorum [gold] [ounce] ss. Pouder of a Lyon's heart [ounce] iv. Filings of a Unicorn's Horn [ounce] ss. Ashes of the whole Chameleon [ounce] iss. Bark of the Witch Hazle Two handfulls. Lumbrici [Earth-worms] A score. Dried Man's Brain [ounce] v. Bruisewort } Egyptian Onions } aa lbss.

Mix the ingredients together and digest in my Spiritus Universalis, with a warm digestion, from the change of the moon to the full, and pass through a fine strainer. This Elixer is temperately hot and moist, Digestive, Lenitive, Dissolutive, Aperative, Strengthening and Glutinative; it opens obstructions, proves Hypnotick and Styptick, is Cardiack, and may become Alexpharmick. It is not specially great for any one Single Distemper, but of much use and benefit in most cases wherein there is difficulty and embarrassment, or that which might be done, doth not so clearly appear manifest and Open to the Eye.

The above elixir is a fine specimen of the product of a shrewd charlatan's fertile brain, and doubtless found a ready sale at an exorbitant price. The fact that one, at least, of its ingredients is mythical, probably enhanced its curative properties, in the minds of a gullible public. The horn of the unicorn was popularly regarded as the most marvellous of remedies. In reality, it was the tusk of a cetaceous animal inhabiting the northern ocean, and known as the sea-unicorn or narwhal. In the popular mind it was of value as an effective antidote against all kinds of poisons, the bites of serpents, various fevers, and the plague.

In describing a scene in the Arctic regions, Josephine Diebitsch Peary wrote as follows in her volume, "The Snow Baby" (1901):

Glossy, mottled seals swim in the water, and schools of narwhal, which used to be called unicorns, dart from place to place, faster than the fastest steam yacht; with their long, white ivory horns, longer than a man is tall, like spears, in and out of the water.

One of the teeth of the narwhal is developed into a straight, spirally fluted tusk, from six to ten feet long, like a horn projecting from the forehead. This horn is sometimes as long as the creature's body, and furnishes a valuable ivory. The narwhal also yields a superior quality of oil.[162:1]

Sir Thomas Browne in his "Pseudo-doxia Epidemica"[162:2] remarked that many specimens of alleged unicorn's horn, preserved in England, were in fact portions of teeth of the Arctic walrus, known as the morse or sea-horse. In northern latitudes these teeth are used as material wherewith to fashion knife-handles or the hilts of swords. The long horns, preserved as precious rarities in many places, are narwhal-tusks.

The belief in the medicinal virtues of unicorn's horn is comparatively modern, as none of the ancients, except the Italian writer 苪 ian (about A. D. 200), ascribed to it any curative or antidotal properties. Sir Thomas Browne characterized this popular superstition of his time as an "insufferable delusion."

H. B. Tristam, in his "Natural History of the Bible," remarks that there is no doubt of the identity of the unicorn of Scripture with the historic urus or aurochs, known also as the re 阮, a strong and large animal of the ox-tribe, having two horns. This animal formerly inhabited Europe, including Great Britain, and survived until comparatively recent times, in Prussia and Lithuania. The belief in the existence of a one-horned quadruped is very ancient. Aristotle mentions as such the oryx or antelope of northern Africa. The aurochs was hunted and killed by prehistoric man, as is shown by the finding of skulls, pierced by flint weapons.[163:1]

In the Septuagint, the Hebrew word re 阮 was translated monoceros in the Greek text. This is alleged by some authorities to be an incorrect rendering. The Vulgate has the Latin term unicornis, the one-horned.

In Lewysohn's "Zoologie des Talmuds" is to be found the following rabbinical legend: When the Ark was ready, and all the creatures were commanded to enter, the re 阮 was unable to pass through the door, owing to its large size. Noah and his sons were therefore obliged to fasten the animal by a rope to the Ark, and to tow it behind. And in order to prevent its being strangled, they attached the rope to its horn, instead of around its neck. . . . It was formerly thought that the legendary unicorn was in reality the one-horned rhinoceros, but this seems improbable. The fabulous creature mentioned by classic writers as a native of India was described as having the size and form of a horse, with one straight horn projecting from its forehead. In the museum at Bristol, England, there is a stuffed antelope from Caffraria, which closely answers this description. Its two straight taper horns are so nearly united that in profile they appear like a single horn.

The unicorn of Heraldry first appeared as a symbol on one of the Anglo-Saxon standards, and was afterwards placed upon the Scottish shield. When England and Scotland were united under James I, the silver unicorn became a supporter of the British shield, being placed opposite the golden lion, in the royal arms of Great Britain.[164:1]

FOOTNOTES:

[155:1] Jonathan Pereira, Selecta e Prescriptis, p. 5.

[156:1] Reusch, Buch der Jubilin, p. 385.

[156:2] Notes and Queries, Tenth Series, June 4, 1904.

[156:3] F. Lenormant, Chaldean Magic, p. 81.

[157:1] Evidence of the old belief in planetary influence is found in our language in the words "jovial," "mercurial," "saturnine," "martial," "disastrous," and "ill-starred."

[158:1] Otto A. Wall, M.D., The Prescription, pp. 12-23. In this work much space is devoted to the history and evolution of medical recipes.

[159:1] Boston Herald, February 27, 1908.

[162:1] The Century Dictionary.

[162:2] Book iii, p. 130.

[163:1] Encyclop鑑ia Britannica, art. "Unicorn"; Rev. J. G. Wood, Bible Animals.

[164:1] F. S. W., Dame Heraldry, p. 175.

CHAPTER XV

REMEDIAL VIRTUES ASCRIBED TO RELICS

A relic has been defined as an object held in reverence or affection, because connected with some sacred or beloved person deceased. And specifically, in the Roman Catholic and Greek churches, a saint's body or portions of it, or an object supposed to have been associated with the life or body of Christ, of the Virgin Mary, or of some saint or martyr, and regarded therefore as a personal memorial, worthy of religious veneration.[165:1]

The worship of relics and the belief in their healing properties appear to have originated in a very ancient custom which prevailed among the early Christians, of assembling at the tombs of martyrs, for the purpose of holding memorial services. The bones of saints also became objects of great veneration, and this doctrine was supported by the teachings of Saint Ambrose, Saint Augustine, Saint Jerome, and other Fathers of the Church, of the fourth and fifth centuries. The belief in the marvellous virtues attributed to sacred relics was sustained by such miracles as that recorded in 2 Kings, xiii, 21: "And it came to pass, as they were burying a man, that, behold, they spied a band of men; and they cast the man into the sepulchre of Elisha; and when the man was let down, and touched the bones of Elisha, he revived, and stood up on his feet."

Some authorities, however, ascribe the origin of the cult of relics to the words contained in Acts, v, 15: "Insomuch that they brought forth the sick into the streets, and laid them on beds and couches, that at the least the shadow of Peter passing by might overshadow some of them."

In the year 325, Saint Helena, the mother of Constantine the Great, the first Christian Emperor of Rome, made a pilgrimage to Jerusalem, where she was alleged to have discovered the wood of the true Cross. This, according to tradition, was found, with two other crosses and various sacred relics, under a temple of Venus, which stood near the Holy Sepulchre. And the true Cross was identified by means of a miraculous test; for when a sick woman was touched with two of the crosses, no effect was apparent; but upon contact with the true Cross, she was immediately restored to health.[166:1] Such is the legend.

Of the four nails found in the place where the Cross was buried, one was said to have been sent to Rome. Another the Empress Helena threw into the Gulf of Venice, to allay a storm; while the other two were sent by her to Constantine, who welded one of them to his helmet, as an amulet, and affixed the other to his horse's headstall.

Among the classic peoples, symbols of their gods were used by physicians in writing prescriptions for material remedies, as invocations or charms, and were credited with the same wonderful healing powers which were ascribed to holy relics, blessed medals and amulets, and in later times to many purely superstitious remedies.[167:1]

The worship of relics naturally afforded a strong impulse to visit sacred places, and especially Palestine.

Generally speaking, the prized relic, a piece of the true cross, whether possessed by a church, a crowned head or a private individual, is a minute speck of wood, scarcely visible to the naked eye, set sometimes on an ivory tablet, and always inclosed in a costly reliquary. M. Rohault de Fleury, who calculates that the total volume of the wood of the original cross must have been somewhere about 178,000,000 cubic millimetres, has made a list of all the relics of which he can find any record, and the sum of their measurements amounts to only 3,941,975 cubic millimetres, or about one forty-fifth of the amount of wood necessary to reconstruct the original cross. In the United States there is not an authenticated relic of the cross as large as half a lead-pencil, and some are so minute as to be visible only through the aid of a microscope. The Church of St. Francis Xavier in New York has a fragment which is exposed for veneration on Easter Sunday, as is the custom in European churches possessing a relic. Another fragment, at the Cathedral, is shown on Good Friday. This relic is in a crystal and gold casket, set with precious stones, which form the centre of a handsome altar cross. The French Church of St. Jean Baptiste, in East Seventy-sixth Street, also possesses a relic of the cross.[168:1]

The powder obtained by scraping the tombstones of saints, when placed in water or wine, was in great repute as a remedy. The French historian, Gregory of Tours (544-595), was said to have habitually carried a box of this powder, when travelling, which he freely dispensed to patients who applied to him.

Great was his faith in this substance, as is apparent from his own words: "Oh, indescribable mixture, incomparable elixir, antidote beyond all praise! Celestial purgative (if I may be permitted to use the expression), which throws into the shade every medical prescription; which surpasses in fragrance every earthly aroma, and is more powerful than all essences; which purges the body like the juice of scammony, clears the lungs like hyssop, and the head like sneezewort; which not only cures the ailing limbs, but also, and this is much more valuable, washes off the stains from the conscience!"[168:2]

Chrysostom (350-407) commented on the fact of the whole world's streaming to the site of Christ's crucifixion. Rome was also a favorite resort of pilgrims, chiefly as the site of the graves of the great apostles, while many flocked to the tomb of Saint Martin of Tours. Meanwhile, wrote Henry C. Sheldon in a "History of the Christian Church," there were emphatic cautions against an overestimate of the value of pilgrimages. The eminent Greek Father, Gregory of Nyssa (332-398), said that change of place brings God no nearer.

The cult of relics developed rapidly in the Middle Ages. Even the theft of these precious objects, we are told, was condoned, "in virtue of the benevolent intent of the thief to benefit the region to which the treasure was conveyed."[169:1] The custom received encouragement from many eminent scholars, who appear to have been deceived by certain mysterious physical phenomena, the nature of which was not understood even in comparatively recent times.[169:2]

Pope Gregory the First (550-604), we are told, was wont to bestow, as a mark of his special favor, presents of keys, in which had been worked up some filings of Saint Peter's chains, accompanied with a prayer that what had bound the apostle for martyrdom, might release the recipient from his sins.

The second Nicene Council (A. D. 787) decreed that no church should be consecrated unless it enshrined some relics.[170:1]

At the celebrated Benedictine abbey of Monte Cassino, in southern Italy, which was founded in the year 529, the care of the sick was enjoined as a pious obligation. There diseases were treated chiefly by means of prayers and conjurations, and by the exposition and application of sacred relics, which appealed to the patients' imagination, and thereby, through suggestion, assisted the healing forces of nature.[170:2]

Thomas Dudley Fosbroke, in "British Monachism," states that among the early monks of England, medical practice devolved on clerks, on account of their ability to read Latin treatises on therapeutics.

Until the middle of the fifteenth century, physicians were forbidden to marry, owing to the prevalent opinion that the father of a family could not heal so well as a bachelor. The art of writing prescriptions was made to conform to the dogmas of the existing religion, "for which reason relics were introduced into the Materia Medica."

The medieval priests and monks, who were actively interested in the development of medical science, encouraged the therapeutic use of such relics. Miraculous agencies were the more eagerly sought after on account of the popular belief in devils and witches as morbiferous creatures.

The reliquary, or repository for relics, was regarded as the most precious ornament in the lady's chamber, the knight's armory, the king's hall of state, and in the apartments of the pope or bishop.[171:1]

Gradually the custom of relic-worship degenerated into idolatry. In the year 1549 John Calvin published a tract on the subject, wherein he stated that the great majority of alleged relics were spurious, and that it could be shown by comparison that each Apostle had more than four bodies, and that every Saint had two or three at least. The arm of Saint Anthony, which had been worshipped at Geneva, when removed from its case, proved to be part of a stag. Among the vast number of precious relics, presumably false, which were exhibited at Rome and elsewhere, were the manger in which Christ was laid at his birth, the pillar on which he leaned, when disputing in the temple, and the waterpots in which he turned water into wine at the marriage feast of Cana at Galilee.[171:2]

FOOTNOTES:

[165:1] Century Dictionary.

[166:1] E. Cobham Brewer, A Dictionary of Miracles, art. "Relics."

[167:1] Otto A. Wall, M.D., The Prescription.

[168:1] Boston Courier, March 26, 1910.

[168:2] Dr. Hugo Magnus, Superstition in Medicine.

[169:1] H. C. Sheldon, op. cit.

[169:2] William Smith and Samuel Cheetham, A Dictionary of Christian Antiquities, art. "Relics."

[170:1] All the Year Round, vol. 69, p. 246; 1891.

[170:2] Time, vol. v; February, 1887.

[171:1] Henry Hart Milman, D.D., History of Latin Christianity, vol. vi, p. 248.

[171:2] Philip Schaff, History of the Christian Church.

CHAPTER XVI

THE HEALING INFLUENCE OF MUSIC

Dubito, an omnia, quae de incantamentis dicuntur carminibusque, non sint adscribenda effectibus musicis, quia excellebant eadem veteres medici. HERMANN BOERHAAVE. (1668-1738.)

Preposterous ass! that never read so far To know the cause why music was ordained. Was it not to refresh the mind of man, After his studies, or his usual pain?-- The Taming of the Shrew, Act III, Scene 1.

I think sometimes, could I only have music on my own terms, could I live in a great city, and know where I could go whenever I wished and get the ablution and inundation of musical waves, that were a bath and medicine. R. W. EMERSON.

Musick, when rightly order'd, cannot be prefer'd too much. For it recreates and exalts the Mind at the same time.

It composes the Passions, affords a strong Pleasure, and excites Nobleness of Thought. . . .

What can be more strange than that the rubbing of a little hair and cat-gut together, should make such a mighty Alteration in a Man that sits at a distance? JEREMY COLLIER, Essay on Music: 1698.

"Music the fiercest grief can charm." POPE, St. Cecilia's Day, I, 118.

From time immemorial the influence of musical sounds has been recognized as a valuable agent in the treatment of nervous affections, and for the relief of various mental conditions. According to one theory, the healing quality of a musical tone is due to its regular periodic vibrations. It acts by substituting its own state of harmony for a condition of mental or physical discord. Noise, being inharmonious, has no curative power. Music may be termed the health and noise the disease of sound.[173:1]

"The man that hath no music in himself," says Shakespeare ("The Merchant of Venice," Act v, Scene 1), "nor is not moved with concord of sweet sounds, is fit for treasons, stratagems, and spoils. The motions of his spirit are dull as night, and his affections dark as Erebus. Let no such man be trusted. . . ."

The ancient Egyptians were not ignorant of musico-therapy. They called music physic for the soul, and had faith in its specific remedial virtues. Music was an accompaniment of their banquets, and in the time of the fourth and fifth dynasties consisted usually of the harmony of three instruments, the harp, flute, and pipe.[173:2] The Persians are said to have cured divers ailments by the sound of the lute. They believed that the soul was purified by music and prepared thereby for converse with the spirits of light around the throne of Ormuzd, the principle of truth and goodness. And the most eminent Grecian philosophers attributed to music important medicinal properties for both body and mind.

John Harrington Edwards, in his volume, "God and Music,"[174:1] remarks that the people of antiquity had much greater faith than the moderns in the efficacy of music as a curative agent in disease of every kind; while the scientific mind of to-day demands a degree of evidence which history cannot furnish, for asserted cures by this means in early times.

Impressed with the sublime nature of music, the ancients ascribed to it a divine origin. According to one tradition, its discovery was due to the sound produced by the wind whistling among the reeds, which grew on the borders of the Nile.

Polybius, the Greek historian of the second century B. C., wrote that music softened the manners of the ancient Arcadians, whose climate was rigorous. Whereas the inhabitants of Cyn 鐡 ha (the modern town of Kalavrita) in the Peloponnesus, who neglected this art, were the most barbarous in Greece. Baron de Montesquieu, in "The Spirit of Laws," remarked that as the popular exercises of wrestling and boxing had a natural tendency to render the ancient Grecians hardy and fierce, there was a necessity for tempering those exercises with others, with a view to rendering the people more susceptible of humane feelings. For this purpose, said Montesquieu, music, which influences the mind by means of the corporeal organs, was extremely proper. It is a kind of medium between manly exercises, which harden the body, and speculative sciences, which are apt to render us unsociable and sour. . . . Let us suppose, for example, a society of men so passionately devoted to hunting as to make it their sole employment; they would doubtless contract thereby a kind of rusticity and fierceness. But if they happened to imbibe a taste for music, we should quickly perceive a sensible difference in their customs and manners. In short, the exercises used by the Greeks could raise but one kind of passions, namely, fierceness, indignation, and cruelty. But music excites all these, and is likewise able to inspire the soul with a sense of pity, lenity, tenderness, and love.

In a rare work, styled "Reflexions on Antient and Modern Music, with the application to the Cure of Diseases,"[175:1] we find that the custom prevailed, among certain nations of old, of initiating their youth into the studies of harmony and music. Whereby, it was believed, their minds became formed to the admiration and esteem of proportion, order, and beauty, and the cause of virtue was greatly promoted. "Music," moreover, "extends the fancy beyond its ordinary compass, and fills it with the gayest images."

Christianus Pazig, in "Magic Incantations," page 29, relates that the wife of Picus, King of Latium, was able by her voice to soothe and appease wild animals, and to arrest the flight of birds.

And the French traveller Villamont asserted that crocodiles were beguiled by the songs of Egyptian fishermen to leave the Nile, and allowed themselves to be led off and exposed for sale in the markets.

Recent experiments have confirmed the traditional theory of the soothing effect of music upon wild animals. A graphophone, with records of Melba, Sembrich, Caruso, and other operatic stars, made the rounds of a menagerie. Many of the larger animals appeared to thoroughly enjoy listening to the melodious strains, which seemed to fascinate them. The one exception, proving the rule, was a huge, blue-faced mandrill, who became enraged at hearing a few bars from "Pagliacci," and tried to wreck the machine. Of all the animals, the lions were apparently the most susceptible to musical influence, and these royal beasts showed an interest in the sweet tones of the graphophone, akin to that of a human melomaniac.[176:1]

There is abundant evidence of the fondness of spiders for soothing musical tones. The insects usually approach by letting themselves down from the ceiling of the apartment, and remain suspended above the instrument.[176:2] Professor C. Reclain, during a concert at Leipsic, witnessed the descent of a spider from a chandelier during a violin solo. But as soon as the orchestra began to play, the insect retreated. Mr. C. V. Boys, who has made some interesting experiments with a view to determining the susceptibility of spiders to the sound of a tuning-fork, reports, in "Body and Mind," that by means of this instrument, a spider may be made to eat what it would otherwise avoid. Male birds charm their mates by warbling, and parrots seem to take delight in hearing the piano played, or in listening to vocal music.

Charles Darwin, in "The Descent of Man," remarks that we can no more explain why musical tones, in a certain order and rhythm, afford pleasure to man and the lower animals, than we can account for the pleasantness of certain tastes and odors. We know that sounds, more or less melodious, are produced, during the season of courtship, by many insects, spiders, fishes, amphibians, and birds. The vocal organs of frogs and toads are used incessantly during the breeding season, and at this time also male alligators are wont to roar or bellow, and even the male tortoise makes a noise.

Music is the sworn enemy of ennui or boredom, and the demons of melancholy. It "hath charms," wrote William Congreve (1670-1729), "to soothe the savage breast."[177:1] Orpheus with his lyre was able to charm wild beasts, and even to control the forces of Nature; and because of its wonderful therapeutic effects, which were well known to the Greeks, they associated Music with Medicine as an attribute of Apollo.[178:1] Chiron the centaur, by the aid of melody, healed the sick, and appeased the anger of Achilles. By the same means the lyric poet Thales, who flourished in the seventh century B. C., acting by advice of an oracle, was able to subdue a pestilence in Sparta.[178:2]

Pythagoras also recognized the potency of music as a remedial force. Tuneful strains were believed by the physicians of old to be uncongenial to the spirits of sickness; but among medicine-men of many American Indian tribes, harsh discordant sounds and doleful chants have long been a favorite means of driving away these same spirits.[178:3] Aulus Gellius, the Roman writer of the second century, in his "Attic Nights,"[178:4] mentioned a traditionary belief that sciatica might be relieved by the soft notes of a flute-player, and quoted the Greek philosopher Democritus (born about B. C. 480) as authority for the statement that the same remedy had power to heal wounds inflicted by venomous serpents. According to Theophrastus, a disciple of Plato and Aristotle (B. C. 374-286), gout could be cured by playing a flute over the affected limb;[179:1] and the Latin author Martianus Capella, who flourished about A. D. 490, asserted that music had been successfully employed in the treatment of fevers, and in quieting the turbulence of drunken revellers.

Among the ancient northern peoples, also, songs and runes were reckoned powerful agents for working good or evil, and were available "to heal or make sick, bind up wounds, stanch blood, alleviate pain, or lull to sleep."[179:2] A verse of an old Icelandic poem, called the "Havamal," whose authorship is accredited to Wodan, runs as follows: "I am possessed of songs, such as neither the spouse of a king nor any son of man can repeat. One of them is called, 'the Helper.' It will help thee at thy need, in sickness, grief, and all adversities. I know a song which the sons of men ought to sing, if they would become skilful physicians."[179:3]

The Anglo-Saxons appreciated the healthful influence of music. At a very early period in their history, a considerable number of persons adopted music and singing as a profession. It was the gleemen's duty to entertain royal personages and the members of their courts. Afterwards these functions devolved upon the minstrels, a class of musicians who wandered from castle to camp, entertaining the nobility and gentry with their songs and accompaniments. The intermediate class of musicians, whom the later minstrels succeeded, appeared in France during the eighth century, and came, at the time of the Norman Conquest, to England, where they were assimilated with the Anglo-Saxon gleemen.[180:1] In the early poetry of Scandinavia there is frequent reference to the magical influence of music. Wild animals are fascinated by the sound of a harp, and vegetation is quickened. The knight, though grave and silent, is attracted, and even though inclined to stay away, cannot restrain his horse.[180:2]

The earliest biblical mention of music as a healing power occurs in Samuel, XVI, 23, where David (the son of Jesse, the Bethlehemite) cured the melancholy of King Saul by playing upon the harp. "So Saul was refreshed, and was well, and the evil spirit departed from him."

In medieval times, music was successfully employed in the treatment of epidemic nervous disorders, a custom which probably originated from the ancient song-remedies or incantations.[180:3] The same agent was also used as an antidote to the poison of a viper's fang, especially the tarantula's bite, which was believed to induce tarantism, or the dancing mania. Antonius Benivenius, a learned Italian physician of the fifteenth century, related that an arrow was drawn from a soldier's body by means of a song.

A notable instance of the power of vocal music in charming away obstinate melancholy is in the case of Philip V of Spain, where the melodious voice of the great Italian singer Farinelli proved effective after all other remedies had failed.

Such are a few instances of the influence of song and melody as seemingly magical agencies, and therefore not inappropriately may they be classed under that branch of folk-lore which deals with healing-spells and verbal medical charms.

It has been well said that music is entitled to a place in our Materia Medica. For while there may not be much music in medicine, there is a great deal of medicine in music. For the latter exerts a powerful influence upon the higher cerebral centres, and thence, through the sympathetic nervous system, upon other portions of the body. Indeed the entire working of the human mechanism, physical and psychical, may be aided by the beautiful art of music. With some people the digestion is facilitated by hearing music.

Voltaire said that this fact accounted for the popularity of the opera.

In such cases the music probably acts by banishing fatigue, which interferes with the proper assimilation of food. Hence one may derive benefit from listening to the orchestra during meal-times at fashionable hotels. Milton believed in the benefit to be derived from listening to music before dinner, as a relief to the mind. And he also recommended it as a post-prandial exercise, "to assist and cherish Nature in her first concoctions, and to send the mind back to study, in good tune and satisfaction." Milton practised what he preached, for it was his custom, after the principal meal of the day, to play on the organ and hear another sing.[182:1]

The Reverend Sydney Smith once said that his idea of heaven was eating foie gras to the sound of trumpets.

There is evidence that in ancient times the banquets, which immediately followed sacrifices, were attended with instrumental music. For we read in Isaiah, v, 12: "And the harp and the viol, the tabret and pipe, and wine, are in their feasts." And in the households of wealthy Roman citizens, instruction was given in the art of carving, to the sound of music, with appropriate gestures, under the direction of the official carver (carptor or scissor).[182:2]

We find in the "Apocrypha"[182:3] the following passage: "If thou be made the master of a feast . . . hinder not musick. . . . A concert of musick in a banquet of wine is as a signet of carbuncle set in gold. As a signet of an emerald set in a work of gold, so is the melody of musick with pleasant wine."

Chaucer, in his "Parson's Tale," speaks of the Curiositie of Minstralcie, at the banquets of the well-to-do in his day.

The banquets of the Anglo-Saxons were enlivened by minstrels and gleemen, whose visits were welcome breaks in the monotony of the people's lives. They added to their musical performances mimicry and other means of promoting mirth, as well as dancing and tumbling, with sleights of hand, and a variety of deceptions to amuse the company.[183:1] In the intervals between the musical exercises, the guests talked, joked, propounded and answered riddles, and boasted of their own exploits, while disparaging those of others. Later, when the liquor took effect, they were wont to become noisy and quarrelsome.[183:2] "Then wine wets the man's breast-passions; suddenly rises clamour in the company, an outcry they send forth various."[183:3]

In the great houses of the nobility and gentry, minstrels' music was the usual seasoning of food. It is true, wrote Mons. J. J. Jusserand, in "English Wayfaring Life of the Fourteenth Century," that "the voices of the singers were at times interrupted by the crunching of the bones, which the dogs were gnawing under the tables, or by the sharp cry of some ill-bred falcon; for many lords kept these favorite birds on perches behind them."

We learn from the same authority that in the great dining-halls of the castles of the wealthy, galleries were placed for the accommodation of the minstrels, above the door of entrance, and opposite to the dais upon which stood the master's table.

FOOTNOTES:

[173:1] Boston Transcript, March 10, 1900.

[173:2] George Rawlinson, History of Ancient Egypt, vol. ii, p. 49.

[174:1] J. G. Millingen, M.D., Curiosities of Medical Experience.

[175:1] London, 1749.

[176:1] Boston Sunday Herald, May 2, 1909.

[176:2] George J. Romanes, Animal Intelligence.

[177:1] The Mourning Bride, Act I, Scene 1.

[178:1] Joseph Ennemoser, The History of Magic, vol. i, p. 358.

[178:2] Music, vol. ix, p. 361; 1896.

[178:3] Daniel G. Brinton, The Myths of the New World, p. 306.

[178:4] Book iv, chap. 13.

[179:1] Larousse, Dictionnaire, art. "Incantation."

[179:2] Brand, Popular Antiquities, vol. iii, p. 1226.

[179:3] M. Mallet, Northern Antiquities, p. 351.

[180:1] Century Dictionary, under "Minstrel."

[180:2] Thomas Keightley, The Fairy Mythology, p. 98.

[180:3] George F. Fort, Medical Economy during the Middle Ages, p. 365.

[182:1] Music, vol. ix; 1896.

[182:2] William Smith, A Dictionary of Greek and Roman Antiquities, art. "Coena."

[182:3] Ecclus. xxxii, 1-6.

[183:1] Joseph Strutt, Sports and Pastimes of the People of England.

[183:2] Thomas Wright, A History of Domestic Manners and Sentiments in England during the Middle Ages.

[183:3] Exeter Manuscript; British Museum.

CHAPTER XVII

THE HEALING INFLUENCE OF MUSIC (CONTINUED)

Dr. Herbert Lilly, in a monograph on musical therapeutics, expresses the opinion that musical sounds received by the auditory nerve, produce reflex action upon the sympathetic system, stimulating or depressing the vaso-motor nerves, and thus influencing the bodily nutrition. He maintains, without fear of contradiction, that certain mental conditions are benefited by suitable musical harmonies. Muscle-fatigue is overcome by stimulating melodies, as is strikingly exemplified in the effect of inspiring martial strains upon wearied troops on the march. And it appears to be an established fact that the complex process of digestion is facilitated by cheerful music, of the kind termed "liver music" by the French, which is provided by them at banquets.[185:1]

But in regard to this subject, there have been not a few scoffers and dissenters, even among people of distinction. Douglas Jerrold, the playwright, was one of these, for he declared that he disliked dining amidst the strains of a military band, because he could taste the brass in his soup. Charles Lamb, in his chapter on "Ears," remarked, that while a carpenter's hammer, on a warm summer day, caused him to "fret into more than midsummer madness," these unconnected sounds were nothing when compared with the measured malice of music. For while the ear may be passive to the strokes of a hammer, and even endure them with some degree of equanimity, to music it cannot be passive. The noted author relates having sat through an Italian opera, till, from sheer pain, he rushed out into the noisiest places of the crowded streets, to solace himself with sounds which he was not obliged to follow, and thus get rid of the distracting torment of endless, fruitless, barren attention! According to his frank avowal, music was to him a source of pain, rather than of pleasure.

The Reverend Richard Eastcott, in his "Sketches of the Origin, Progress and Effects of Music," told of a "gentleman of very considerable understanding," who was heard to declare that the rattling of a fire-pan and tongs was as grateful to his feelings as the best concert he ever heard. However, such rare exceptions, if not germane to our subject, may be said to prove the general rule that music is of real value in therapeutics, and that most people are susceptible to its beneficent influences.

Music has accomplished a great many things and has been put to many uses, but it is seldom employed in making good boys out of bad.

An almost accidental experiment at the Middlesex County truant school at North Chelmsford has shown it to be a truth, that wickedness takes flight at martial strains; for a full-fledged brass band, in which the delinquent youths are the musicians, has fairly revolutionized the discipline of the school, and many a lad who did not have half a chance has been started "right" on the road to success.

The question is often asked: How can music effect a character-metamorphosis in the boy who has every mental and moral indication of turning out badly?

Music is an educative factor of prime importance, and promotes the evolution of good hereditary traits. Whatever the psychologic explanation of its effects may be, it appears to develop the qualities of kindness and manliness.[187:1]

Not every one, however, is influenced by the foregoing considerations. A recent writer, in an essay on the "Plague of Music," remarks that under the name of music we are afflicted with every variety of noise; for example, the sounds produced by hurdy-gurdies, bag-pipes and minstrels; the harpman, the lady who has seen better days, and who sings before our house in the evening. "Not to mention the millions of pianos and the millions of fiddles that never cease being thumped and scratched all the world over, night and day. The contemplation of such collective discord is truly appalling."[188:1]

The famous English philosopher, Roger Bacon (1214-1292), known as "The Admirable Doctor," wrote that a cheerful mind brings power and vigor, makes a man rejoice, stirs up Nature, and helps her in her actions and motions; of which sort are joy, mirth, and whatever provokes laughter, as also instrumental music and songs, facetious conversation, and observation of the celestial bodies.

It has been proved, by physiological experiments upon men and the lower animals, that musical sounds produce a marked effect upon the circulation. The pulse-rate is usually quickened, and the force of the heart-beats increased in varying degrees, dependent upon the pitch, intensity and timbre of the sounds, and the idiosyncrasy of the individual.[188:2]

It may be safely affirmed, therefore, that music should have a place among psychic remedial agents.

A recent writer has remarked that the "Marsellaise" was like wine to the French revolutionists, and lifted many a head, and straightened many a weary back on some of those terrible forced marches of Napoleon's.

Music may be classed in the same category with certain drugs, as a therapeutic agent. And like drugs, each composition has its own special effect. Thus a brisk Strauss waltz might act as a stimulant, but it would not answer as a narcotic. A nocturne would be sure to soothe.[189:1]

The time may come when a German street-band will be recognized as a powerful tonic; a cornet solo will take the place of a blister; a symphony or a sonata may be recommended instead of morphine; the moxa will give way to Wagner, and opium to Brahms. A prolonged shake by a singer will drive out chills and fever, according to the theory of Hahnemann. Cots at symphony concerts may yet command the highest premiums.[189:2]

Music is one of those intangible but effective aids of Medicine, which exert their healthful influence through the nervous system. It is in fact a mental tonic. A writer in the London "Lancet" remarks that "a pleasing and lively melody can awake in a faded brain the strong emotion of hope, and energizing by its means the languid nerve control of the whole circulation, strengthen the heart-beat and refresh the vascularity of every organ. Even aches are soothed for a time by a transference of attention, and why then should not pain be lulled by music?"

Robert Burton, author of "The Anatomy of Melancholy," in commenting on the curative effects of music, remarked that it is a sovereign remedy against mental depression, capable even of driving away the Devil himself.

"When griping grief the heart doth wound, And doleful dumps the mind oppress, Then music with her silver sound, With speedy help doth lend redress." Romeo and Juliet, Act IV, Scene 5.

The nurse's song, Burton wrote, makes a child quiet, and many times, the sound of a trumpet on a sudden, bells ringing, a carman's whistle, a boy singing some ballad on the street, alters, revives and recreates a restless patient who cannot sleep in the night. Many men are made melancholy by hearing music, but the melancholy is of a pleasing kind.

In a curious German treatise, "Der Musikalische Arzt,"[190:1] we find the following quotation from an article entitled "Reflections on Ancient and Modern Music."[190:2]

"If it be demanded how musick becomes a remedy, and inciteth the patient to dance, 'tis answer'd that sound having a great influence upon the actions of the air, the air mov'd causeth a like motion in the next air, and so on till the like be produced in the Spirits of the body, to which the air is impelled."

According to the French physician, Jean Etienne Dominique Esquirol (1772-1840), music acts upon the physique by determining nervous vibrations, and by exciting the circulation. It acts upon the morale by fixing the attention upon sweet impressions, and by calling up agreeable recollections.

Francis Fournier de Pescay, a contemporary of the above-named, commented on the fact that many famous writers of antiquity regarded music as a panacea, whereas in the light of modern medical science, it cannot be considered as an effective remedy in such affections as rheumatism, for example.[191:1]

An adagio may set a gouty father to sleep, and a capriccio may operate successfully on the nerves of a valetudinary mother. A slight indisposition may be removed by a single air, while a more obstinate case may require an overture or a concerto. The tastes of the patient should be consulted.

Country squires, when kept indoors by stress of bad weather, will experience much relief in a hunting-song, while young gentlemen of the town will perhaps prefer an old English derry-down. Hospital inmates will usually be content with hurdy-gurdies, and the poorer classes may be supplied with ballads at their own homes. Some patients will recover with all the rapidity of a jig, while others will mend in minuet-time. And surely the public welfare will be eminently promoted, when our physicians' prescriptions are printed from music-type, and when we have nothing more nauseous to swallow than the words of a modern opera.[192:1]

According to the Dutch physician Lemnius (1505-1568), music is a chief antidote against melancholy; it revives the languishing soul, affecting not only the ears, but the vital and animal spirits. It erects the mind, and makes it nimble.

The Reverend Sydney Smith graphically described the effect of enlivening music upon an audience, who had been manifestly bored and were gaping with ennui during the execution of an elaborate fugue, by a skilled orchestra. Suddenly there sprang up a lively little air, expressive of some natural feeling. And instantly every one beamed with satisfaction, and was ready to aver that music affords the most delightful and rational entertainment.

And such is doubtless the opinion of the great majority of people of culture and refinement, especially those of a jovial or mercurial temperament. According to Martin Luther, the Devil is a saturnine person, and music is hateful to him.

Many and sundry are the means, says Robert Burton, which philosophers and physicians have prescribed to exhilarate a sorrowful heart, to divert those fixed and intent cares and meditations, which in this malady so much offend; but in my judgment, none so present, none so powerful, none so apposite as mirth, music and merry company.[193:1]

During recent years the influence of music in disease has been the subject of renewed attention. In London Canon Harford, an enthusiastic believer in the efficacy of this method of treatment, organized bands of musicians, under the auspices of the Order of Saint Cecilia, who visited certain hospitals, where permission had been given, and there exercised their art with results highly encouraging and beneficial.

And in Boston Dr. John Dixwell has for many years been active in providing music for hospital patients. His admirable enterprise has been successful, and has received the endorsement of the medical fraternity. A wise discrimination is essential in the selection of music especially adapted to benefit any particular class of cases.

The National Society of Musical Therapeutics was founded in the city of New York, by Miss Eva Augusta Vescelius, in the year 1903, with the object of encouraging the study of music in relation to life and health; and also for the promotion of its use as a curative agent in hospitals, asylums, and prisons. The therapeutic use of music is believed to have passed the experimental stage. It is now admitted, says Miss Vescelius, that music can be so employed as to exercise a distinct psychological influence upon the mind, nerve-centres and circulatory system; and may serve as an efficient remedy for many ills to which the flesh is said to be heir. The selection of music in hospitals and asylums needs thoughtful consideration, for there we meet with all kinds of discord. An emotional song, for example, which would give pleasure to one, might sadden another, and a patient suffering from nostalgia would not be benefited by a melody suggesting a home-picture.

Will the trained nurse of the future have to include voice culture in her training before she is declared competent to minister to the wants of the sick?

This question is raised by Dr. George M. Stratton, professor of experimental psychology in Johns Hopkins University. In an address on "The Nature and Training of the Emotions," delivered before more than a hundred nurses of the hospitals of Baltimore, he made the broad statement that music would be a vital factor in treating the sick in the future.

Dr. Stratton did not insist that every nurse of the future must be a Patti, a Melba, or a Nordica; but he held that in the future a young woman who devotes her life to nursing the sick should be able to sing to the patient under her care.[194:1]

The mental effect of music is generally recognized as beneficial, in that it lifts the entire being into a higher state. That this effect is communicated to the body, is admitted, but the extent of physical benefit has not been sufficiently investigated either by musicians or by scientists. In the application of music for the treatment of disease, it should be remembered that the seat of many disorders is primarily in the mind, and that therefore the mental condition must be radically changed before a cure is possible. "In listening to music, the mind absorbs those tones which have become silenced in itself, and in the body as a necessary consequence; just as the stomach assimilates those food-elements which are required to repair the waste of the system. Thus our music-food is selected and distributed where it is most needed, and this natural selection of musical vibrations acts specifically upon those parts of the body which are out of harmony. A concert programme is a menu for the multitude. We hear all the music printed on it, but digest very little of it. Some kinds of music thus heard, must inevitably be wasted on the listener, or cause a musical dyspepsia."[195:1]

The English clergyman and writer, Hugh Reginald Haweis, extols music as a healthy outlet for emotion, and as especially adapted for young ladies. Joy flows naturally into ringing harmonies, says he, while music has the subtle power to soften melancholy, by presenting it with its fine emotional counterpart.

A good play on the piano has not unfrequently taken the place of a good cry upstairs, and a cloud of ill-temper has often been dispersed by a timely practice. One of Schubert's friends used to say that, although very cross before sitting down to his piano, a long scramble-duet through a symphony or through one of his own delicious and erratic pianoforte duets, always restored him to good humor.[196:1]

For many years the subject of musico-therapy has been discussed editorially in the columns of the "London Lancet." We give some statements emanating from this authority.

Music influences both brain and heart through the spinal cord, probably on account of its vibratory or wave motion, which stimulates the nerve-centres. . . .

It acts as a refreshing mental stimulant and restorative. Therefore it braces depressed nervous tone and indirectly through the nervous system reaches the tissues. It is of most use in depressed mental conditions. . . . The value of music as a therapeutic agent cannot yet be precisely stated, but it is no quack's nostrum. It is an intangible, but effective aid of medicine.

It seems strange that the healing influence of music has not been more thoroughly studied from a psychological standpoint, and utilized, when one is mindful of the great store of evidence, gathered for centuries, of the marked power of this agent upon the lower animals, and of its worth as a mental, and therefore as a physical tonic and stimulant, for human beings. A chief reason for this neglect has been ascribed to the materialistic views which have prevailed in therapeutics.

It was formerly believed quite generally, in Italy and elsewhere, that music was the only efficient cure for the effects of the bite of the tarantula, a species of large spider, so called from the city of Taranto. These effects consisted of a feigned or imaginary disease known as tarantism, which was prevalent in Apulia and other portions of southern Italy during the sixteenth and seventeenth centuries. Tarantism was an epidemic nervous affection characterized by involuntary dancing, gesticulations, contortions and cries. In spite, however, of all that has been written on this subject by physicians and historians, it appears to be a fact that the bite of the tarantula is not more venomous than that of other large spiders. Indeed, Dr. H. Chomet, who diligently investigated the matter, never succeeded in finding a case of tarantism, nor was he able even to obtain a glimpse of one of these insects.

It is certain, however, that tarantism was very prevalent in earlier times. J. F. C. Hecker, M.D., in his "Epidemics of the Middle Ages," stated that the music of the flute, cithern or other instrument alone afforded relief to patients affected with this disease. So common was it, that the cities and villages of Apulia resounded with the beneficent strains of fifes, clarinets and drums. And the superstition was general that by means of music and dancing, the poison of the tarantula was distributed over the whole body, and was then eliminated through the pores of the skin.

The bite of the star-lizard, Stellio vulgaris, of Southern Europe, was also popularly believed to be poisonous.

According to Perotti (1430-1480), persons who had been bitten by this reptile fell into a state of melancholia and stupefaction. While in this condition they were very susceptible to the influence of music. At the very first tone of a favorite melody, they sprang up, shouting for joy, and danced without intermission until they sank to the ground, exhausted.

Frequent allusions to the remarkable therapeutic power of music, and especially to its specific anti-toxic virtues, are to be found in the works of many writers. Sir Philip Sidney (1554-1586), in "Arcadia," book 1, said: "This word did not less pierce poor Pyrocles, than the right tune of music toucheth him that is sick of the tarantula." And Jonathan Swift (1667-1745), in "The Tale of a Tub," has this passage: "He was troubled with a disease, reversed to that called the stinging of the tarantula, and would run dog-mad at the noise of music, especially a pair of bag-pipes." Again: "This Malady has been removed, like the Biting of a Tarantula, with the sound of a musical instrument."[199:1]

Many physicians and historians have written on this subject, and with singular unanimity have endorsed music as a curative agent for tarantism.

Notable among these were Alexander ab Alexandro, a prominent Neapolitan civilian, who flourished toward the close of the fifteenth century, and Athanasius Kircher, a famous German Jesuit, in a treatise entitled "Ars Magnetica de Tarantismo" (Rome, 1654). Dr. Richard Mead, in an essay on the tarantula, published in 1702, wrote that this insect was wont to creep about in the Italian corn-fields during the summer months, and at that season its bite was especially venomous. Music was the sole remedy employed, and none other was needed. Among other authorities may be mentioned: Dr. Pierre Jean Burette (1665-1747), "Dialogue sur la musique"; Dr. Giorgio Baglivi, "De Anatomia, Morsu et Effectibus Tarantulae Dissertatio" (1695); and Dr. Th 閙 dore Craanen, a Dutch physician, "Tractatus physico-medicus De Tarantula" (Naples, 1722). Worthy of note also is an elaborate dissertation, "System einer Medizinischen Musik" (Bonn, 1835), by Dr. Peter Joseph Schneider, wherein the author devotes several pages to this interesting theme.

Dr. Mead, above mentioned, gave a curious description of the symptoms of tarantism. "While the patients are dancing," said he, "they lose in a manner the use of all their senses, like so many drunkards, and indulge in many ridiculous and foolish antics. They talk and act rudely, and take great pleasure in playing with vine-leaves, naked swords, red cloths, and the like. They have a particular aversion for anything of a black color, so that if a bystander happens to appear in apparel of that hue, he must immediately withdraw; otherwise the patients relapse into their symptoms with as much violence as ever."

FOOTNOTES:

[185:1] New York Medical Record, October 29, 1909.

[187:1] Boston Daily Advertiser, November 7, 1907.

[188:1] Mrs. John Lane, The Champagne Standard.

[188:2] Chambers's Journal, vol. lxxi, p. 145; 1894.

[189:1] Appleton's Booklovers' Magazine, July, 1905.

[189:2] Boston Herald, May 12, 1907.

[190:1] Wien (Vienna), 1807.

[190:2] Philosophical Transactions, 1668, p. 662.

[191:1] The Lancet, vol. ii; 1880.

[192:1] The Gentleman's Magazine, vol. lxxvii; November, 1807.

[193:1] Anatomy of Melancholy, vol. ii, p. 132.

[194:1] The Chicago Inter-Ocean.

[195:1] Boston Transcript, March 10, 1900.

[196:1] Music and Morals.

[199:1] The Spectator, August 18, 1714.

CHAPTER XVIII

QUACKS AND QUACKERY

Quackery and the love of being quacked, are in human nature as weeds are in our fields. DR. J. BROWN, Spare Hours.

They are Quack-salvers, Fellowes that live by senting oyles and drugs. BEN JONSON, Volpone, Act II, Scene 2.

These, like quacks in Medicine, excite the malady to profit by the cure, and retard the cure to augment the fees. WASHINGTON IRVING.

Here also they have, every night in summer, a world of Montebanks,

Ciarlatani, and such stuff, who together with their remedies, strive to please the People with their little Comedies, Popet-plays and songs. R. LASSELS, Voy. Ital.: 1698.

Le monde n'a jamais manqu?de charlatans; cette science, de tout temps, fut en professeurs fertile. LA FONTAINE.

He took himself to be no mean Doctour, who being guilty of no Greek, and being demanded why it was called an hectic fever; 'because,' saith he, 'of an hecking cough, which ever attendeth that disease.' THOMAS FULLER, The Holy State.

Man is a dupable animal. Quacks in Medicine, quacks in Religion, and quacks in Politics know this and act upon that knowledge. There is scarcely anyone who may not, like a trout, be taken by tickling. ROBERT SOUTHEY.

Quack doctors are indeed pompous, self-sufficient, affectedly solemn, venal and unfeeling with a vengeance. VICESIMUS KNOX, D.D.

If Satan has ever succeeded in compressing a greater amount of concentrated mendacity into one set of human bodies, above every other description, it is in the advertising quacks. Pacific Medical and Surgical Journal.

The bold and unblushing assertion of the empiric, of a never-failing remedy, constantly reiterated, inspires confidence in the invalid, and not unfrequently tends by its operation on the mind, to assist in the eradication of disorder. THOS. J. PETTIGREW, F.R.S.

The word quack, meaning a charlatan, is an abbreviation of quack-salver. To quack is to utter a harsh, croaking sound, like a duck; and hence secondarily, to talk noisily and to make vain and loud pretensions.[202:1] And a salver is one who undertakes to perform cures by the application of ointments or cerates. Hence the term quack-salver was commonly used in the seventeenth century, signifying an ignorant person, who was wont to extol the curative virtues of his salves. Now we see, said Francis Bacon, in "The Advancement of Learning,"[202:2] the weakness and credulity of men. For they will often prefer a mountebank or witch before a learned physician. And therefore the poets were clear-sighted in discerning this extreme folly, when they made

Esculapius and Circe brother and sister. For in all times, in the opinion of the multitude, witches, old women and impostors have had a competition with physicians.

According to one authority, the term quack is derived from an ancient Saxon word, signifying small, slender and trifling, and hence was applied to shallow and frivolous itinerant peddlers, who foisted upon a credulous community such wares as penny-plasters, balsam of liquorice for coughs, snuffs for headaches, and infallible eye-lotions.[203:1]

It has also been maintained that quack is a corruption of quake, and that quack-doctors were so called because, in marshy districts, patients affected with intermittent fever, sometimes vulgarly known as the quakes, were wont to be treated by ignorant persons, who professed to charm away the disease, and hence were styled quake-doctors.

In William Harrison's "Description of the Island of Britain," occurs the following curious passage: "Now we have many chimneys, and yet our tenderlings complain of reumes, catarres and poses; then had we none but reredores, and our heads did never ake. For, as the smoke in those days was supposed to be a sufficient hardening for the timber of the house, so it was reputed a far better medicine to keep the good man and his family from the quacke or pose, wherewith as then very few were acquainted." A writer in "Notes and Queries,"[203:2] remarked that the word quacke, in the foregoing extract, probably signified a disease rather than a charlatan, and possibly the mysterious affection known as "the poofs," from which good Queen Bess suffered one cold winter. This quacke appears to have been a novelty and therefore fashionable, affected by the tenderlings of that era, "as the proper thing to have." The quack-doctor, continues the writer above mentioned, must have been a fashionable style of man, not meddling much with the poor, and familiar with boudoirs, curing the new disease with new and wondrous remedies.

May not the word quacke, asks Stylites, another enquirer, as above used, mean quake or ague? For an ague-doctor must have had much employment, and if successful, great renown, in those days of fens, marshes and undrained ground.

In an anniversary discourse delivered before the New York Academy of Medicine, November 7, 1855, Dr. John Watson remarked that the numbers and pretensions of the illegitimate sons of Esculapius were as great in ancient as in modern times. And they were quite as wont to receive the patronage of the upper classes. The Emperor Nero thus favored the shrewd Lydian practitioner, Thessalus, who maintained that all learning was without value.

And if we may believe the statements of Pliny and Galen, the Roman quacks equalled, if they did not exceed, in ignorance and arrogance, the vast horde of handicraftsmen, bone-setters, herniotomists, lithotomists, abortionists, and poison-venders, who overran Southern Europe throughout the Middle Ages.

The inhabitants of ancient Chaldea, in common with many primitive peoples of later times, cherished the belief that all diseases were caused by demons. Medicine was merely a branch of Magic, and the chief healing agents were exorcisms, incantations, and enchanted beverages. There were, properly speaking, no physicians. Sometimes, wrote Francis Lenormant, in "Chaldean Magic," disease was regarded as an effect of the wickedness of different demons, and sometimes it appears to have been considered as the work of a distinct malevolent being, who exercised his power upon man.

According to the old Shamanic belief, which was the primeval religion of all mankind, every physical ailment is caused by a little devil which enters the body and can be expelled therefrom only by means of magic.

Abundant traces of this doctrine, says Charles Godfrey Leland in "Gipsy Sorcery," appear in our highest civilization and religion among people who gravely attribute every evil to the Devil, instead of to the unavoidable antagonisms of nature. "If," continues this writer, "a pen drops from our fingers, or a penny rolls from our grasp, the former, of course, falls on our new white dress, while the latter, nine times out of ten, goes directly to the nearest grating, crack or rat-hole."

In the religion of the ancient Copts, the Devil was believed to have inherited from his ancestors all the power attributed by ignorance and superstition to certain superior beings. He it was who originated all diseases, and by a singular contradiction, he likewise cured them, either directly or through the agency of the magicians and quacks who followed in his train.[206:1]

According to a widespread doctrine of antiquity, innumerable demons were ever active in endeavoring to inflict diseases upon the bodies of human beings.

No medical practitioner, however skilful, could successfully cope with these supernatural beings. Their evil designs could be checked only by experts in occult science. It has been said that whoever humors the credulity of man, is sure to prosper. The modern quack exemplifies this. "The Devil, the Christian successor of the ancient evil spirit, has exerted a great influence on the medical views of all classes of people. He and his successors were considered 'the disturbers of the peace' in the health of humanity. The Devil was able to influence each individual organ in a manner most disagreeable to the owner of the same."[206:2] Although the hideous portrayals of the Evil One, with horns, hoofs, pitchfork, and tail, appealed strongly to the imagination, they were wholly fanciful. If Satan were to appear in human form, as for example in the guise of a charlatan (says William Ramsey in "The Depths of Satan," 1889), we might expect him to assume the appearance, dress and demeanor of a gentleman.

Indeed, although the idea of the embodiment of evil is naturally repellent, a study of the Devil's personality, as represented in theology, romance, and popular tradition, reveals much that is interesting. In the role of a medical pretender, however, he deserves no more sympathy than any other quack.

In England, says William George Black, in "Folk-Medicine," the Devil has long represented much of the paganism still existing, and seems to have been regarded almost as the head of the medical profession. He has enjoyed the reputation of being able to inflict and cure diseases, not only those of his own production, but also natural diseases, since he knows their origin and causes better than physicians can. For, wrote the learned Dutch practitioner and demonologist, Johann Wier (1515-1588), physicians being younger than the Devil, must necessarily have had less experience.

James Grant, in the "Mysteries of All Nations" (page 1), remarks that the doctrine of devils is of great antiquity, probably dating from the Creation.

The immediate descendants of Adam and Eve must have learned from them, or by tradition, the circumstances connected with the temptation, fall, and expulsion from the Garden of Eden. Therefore it seems highly probable that the serpent was regarded, at a very early period, as something more than an ordinary earthly reptile.

In the Dark Ages popular opinion credited the Devil with a vast amount of erudition; and he was, moreover, reputed to be well versed in medical science and magical arts. Whenever a man of genius had accomplished some task which appeared to be above the powers of the human mind, it was commonly believed that the Devil either had performed the work or had at least rendered some assistance.[208:1]

Burton quotes from the German philosopher, Nicholas Taurellus (born 1547), as follows: "Many doubt whether the Devil can cure such diseases as he hath not made; and some flatly deny it. Howsoever, common experience confirms to our astonishment that magic can work such facts, and that the Devil without impediment can penetrate through all the parts of our bodies, and cure such maladies by means to us unknown."

Again, says Burton, many famous cures are daily performed, affording evidence that the Devil is an expert physician; and God oftentimes permits witches and magicians to produce these effects. Paracelsus encouraged his patients to cultivate a strong imagination, whereby they should experience beneficial results. . . . Therein lies the secret in a nutshell. If a man has confidence in the treatment prescribed by a charlatan, he may be benefited thereby. The Devil is a charlatan. Therefore, if God permit, even diabolical remedies may be efficacious, if the patient's faith in them is strong enough. It is not so much the quality as the strength of the faith, says Dr. McComb in "Religion and Medicine," that is of vital moment, so far as the removal of a given disorder is concerned.

The Christians of the early centuries accepted the pagan doctrine of demonology without modification. The belief in demoniac possession and the belief in witches were later developments from this same doctrine. In the third century originated a new order of ecclesiastics, whose members were known as exorcists. The expulsion of evil spirits was their special function. But in addition to the official exorcists, many sorcerers and magicians assumed to cure the possessed, as well as those suffering from other diseases. The idea of good and evil demons assumed in the Middle Ages a specifically Christian character, which resembled the ancient Babylonian doctrine except that the good demons were replaced by angels and saints, whereas the evil spirits were embodied in the Devil. Both saints and devils were thenceforth destined to play their part in the domain of medicine.

Martin Luther, as is well known, was a firm believer in the doctrine which held that the Devil was the originator of all diseases. No ailment, maintained the great reformer, comes from God, who is good, and does good to every one. It is the Devil who causes and performs all mischief, who interferes with all play and all arts, and who brings about pestilences and fevers. Luther believed that he himself was compelled, when his physical condition was out of order, to have a scuffle with the Evil One, and thereby obtain the mastery over him.[210:1]

Tatian, the Syrian writer, of the second century, declared that the profligacy of demons had made use of the productions of nature for evil purposes. The demons, he wrote, do not cure, but by their art make men their captives.

In that age, everybody, of whatever class or station in life, believed in the existence of demons, who were thought to be omnipresent, infesting men and the lower animals, as well as trees and rivers. At the time of the Reformation the same belief prevailed and was an important factor in influencing men's actions.[210:2]

A belief in the personality of the Evil One is amply warranted by Scripture. What is not warranted, says a writer in "Social England,"[210:3] by anything in Holy Writ, is the medieval conception of Satan, ruling over a kingdom of darkness, in rivalry with God.

Ignorance is guided by terror, rather than by love. To the undisciplined mind, whatever is supernatural or unexpected, makes a stronger appeal than the familiar phenomena of daily life. We cannot understand the motives and acts of our forefathers, wrote Henry C. Lea, in a "History of the Inquisition of the Middle Ages," unless we take into consideration the mental condition engendered by the consciousness of a daily and hourly personal contact with Satan.

Charlatans were not unknown in the fifth century B. C. For the great Hippocrates inveighed against those who relied on amulets and charms as curative agents. In his view, the physician should possess a mind of such serenity and dignity as to be superior to superstition, for the latter is incompatible with a knowledge of the truth.[211:1]

The Romans of old, who drove nails into the walls of the Temple of Jupiter, in the hope of warding off the Plague, employed thereby a quack remedy.

Indeed, for more than six hundred years, they had no physicians, but employed theurgic methods of treatment by means of prayers, charms, and prescriptions from the ancient Sibylline Books, which were reputed to date from the reign of Tarquin the Proud, in the sixth century B. C. These volumes were kept in a stone chest, under ground, in the Temple of Jupiter Capitolinus at Rome. The ancient Romans possessed only the rude surgery and domestic medicine of the barbarians, until the importation of scientific methods from Greece. Cato the Censor (B. C. 234-149) disliked physicians, partly because they were mostly Greeks, and partly because he himself, although venerated as a model of Roman virtue, was an outrageous quack, who thought himself equal to a whole college of physicians.[212:1]

From a very early time, and for many centuries, medical pretenders and empirics were known as "magicians." Practitioners of this class throve exceedingly during the reigns of several Roman emperors. They strove to work upon the imaginations of the people by sensational curative methods. Inasmuch, wrote Dr. Hugo Magnus, as whatever is curious and unusual, has always possessed a special fascination for humanity, the incredible remedies of the magicians found everywhere hosts of believers. And as the most nonsensical theories, if well tinged with the miraculous, find eager credence, there developed a rude form of psycho-therapy. For by the employment of extraordinary and even loathsome substances, many of which had no value as material remedies, they sought to impress curative ideas upon the minds of their patients, and doubtless very often with success. Inventive genius must have been sorely taxed among the magicians, in their endeavors to originate sensational prescriptions. The voluminous works of Alexander of Tralles, Quintus Serenus Samonicus, Marcellus Empiricus, and of many others, show how close was the union between medicine and magic. An enumeration of uncouth remedies formerly in vogue would fill huge pharmacopoeias, and belongs to the domain of Folk-Medicine. Let one or two examples suffice here.

For the removal of those hardened portions of the epidermis, usually occurring upon the feet, and vulgarly known as corns, Pliny the Elder, in his "Natural History," recommends the sufferer, after observing the flight of a meteor, to pour a little vinegar upon the hinge of a door.

And Sextus Placitus Papyriensis, a nonsensical medical writer of the fourth century, advises, for the cure of glaucoma, that the affected eye be rubbed with the corresponding organ of a wolf.

Dr. Theodor Puschmann, in his "History of Medical Education," quotes an old writer[213:1] who inveighed against those practitioners who were wont to fill the ears of their patients with stories of their own professional skill, while depreciating the services of others of the fraternity. Such unscrupulous quacks sought also to win over the patient's friends by little attentions, flatteries and innuendoes. Many, said this philosopher, recoil from a man of skill even, if he is a braggart. "When the doctor," he continues, "attended by a man known to the patient, and having a right of entry into the house, advances into the dwelling of the sick man, he should make his appearance in good clothes, with an inclination of the head; he should be thoughtful and of good bearing, and observe all possible respect. So soon as he is within, word, thought and attention should be given to nothing else but the examination of the patient, and whatever else appertains to the case."

In England, during the earliest times, the administration of medicines was always attended with religious ceremonial, such as the repetition of a psalm. These observances however were often tinctured with a good deal of heathenism, the traditional folk-lore of the country, in the form of charms, magic and starcraft. It is evident, wrote the author of "Social England,"[214:1] from the cases preserved by monkish chronicles, that the element of hysteria was prominent in the maladies of the Middle Ages, and that these affections were therefore peculiarly susceptible to psychic treatment. The Angles and Saxons brought with them to England a belief in medicinal runes and healing spells, and the cures wrought by their medical men were attributed to the magic potency of the charms employed. Some interesting information on contemporary manners is contained in a "Book of Counsels to Young Practitioners" (A. D. 1300). The use of polysyllabic and unintelligible words is therein recommended, probably as a goad to the patient's imagination.

Medical charms, wrote a shrewd philosopher of old, are not to be used because they can effect any change, but because they bring the patient into a better frame of mind.[215:1]

An interesting account of the manners and methods of itinerant charlatans of the period is found in "English Wayfaring Life in the Middle Ages" (fourteenth century), by the noted writer and diplomat, M. Jean Jules Jusserand. These Bohemian mountebanks went about the world, selling health. They selected the village green or market-place as headquarters, and spreading a carpet or piece of cloth on the ground, proceeded to harangue the populace. Big words, marvellous tales, praise of their own distinguished ancestry, enumeration of the wonderful cures wrought by themselves, statements of their purely altruistic motives and benevolent designs, and of their contempt for filthy lucre, these were characteristic features of their discourses, which preceded the exhibition and sale of infallible nostrums.

The law, wrote M. Jusserand, distinguished very clearly between an educated physician and a cheap-jack of the cross-ways. The court-doctor, for example, had the support of an established reputation. He had studied at one of the universities, and he offered the warranty of his high position. The wandering herbalist was less advantageously known. In the country, indeed, he was usually able to escape the rigor of the laws, but in the cities and larger towns he could not ply his trade with impunity. The joyous festivals of Old England attracted many of these hawkers of pills and elixirs, for on such occasions they met the rustic laborers, whose simplicity rendered them an easy prey. These peasant-folk pressed around, open-mouthed, uncertain whether they ought to laugh or to be afraid. But they finished usually by buying specimens of the eloquently vaunted cure-alls.

In medieval times, we are told, it was difficult to distinguish quacks from skilled practitioners, because the latter were inclined to be superstitious. In the year 1220 the University of Paris, with the sanction of the Church and municipality, issued a statute against unlicensed practitioners, and in 1271 another, whereby Jews and Jewesses were forbidden "to practice medicine or surgery on any Catholic Christian." All so-called chirurgeons and apothecaries, as well as herbalists, of either sex, were enjoined from visiting patients, performing operations, or prescribing any medicines except certain confections in common use, unless in the presence and under the direction of a physician, the penalties being excommunication, imprisonment, and fine.[216:1]

Never before, says Roswell Park, M.D., in "An Epitome of the History of Medicine," were there so many sorcerers, astrologers and alchemists, as existed at the close of the Dark Ages. These were mostly restless adventurers, of a class common at all periods of history, who chafed under the yoke of authority. Such individuals, in enlisting in the army of charlatans, were not usually actuated by philanthropic motives. Whatever benevolent sentiments they may have entertained, were in behalf of themselves. Many of them lived apart, as recluses, and were, in modern parlance, cranks, who lacked mental poise. Yet they were usually shrewd, and more or less adepts in occult science.

The power of auto-suggestion was evident in the cures of medieval ailments wrought by the methods of faith-healing. Prayer and intercession were the chief means employed, but these were often supplemented by the use of concoctions of medicinal herbs from the monastery garden.

The resources of therapeutics were, moreover, derived from a strange mixture of magic, astrology, and alchemy. A contemporary manual of "Hints to Physicians" advised the doctor, when called to visit a patient, to recommend himself to God, and to the Archangel Raphael. Then, after having refreshed himself with a drink, he was to praise the beauty of the country and the liberality of the family. He was also cautioned to avoid expressing a hasty opinion of the case, because the patient's friends would attach the more value to the physician's judgment, if they were obliged to wait for it.[218:1]

Paracelsus devoted much attention to chemistry as a science distinct from alchemy. Indeed he may be regarded as the founder of medical chemistry.[218:2] He extolled the merits of certain medicines now recognized as among the most valuable in the modern pharmacopoeia. Chief among these was the tincture of opium, to which he gave its present name of laudanum, a contraction of laudandum, something to be praised.

The eccentric German alchemist and philosopher, Henry Cornelius Agrippa (1486-1535), described a prosperous charlatan of his day as "clad in brave apparel, and having on his fingers showy rings, glittering with precious stones; a fellow who had gotten fame on account of his travels in far countries, and by reason of his obstinate manner of vaunting with stiff lies the merits of his nostrums. Such an one had continually in his mouth many barbarous and uncouth words."

Towards the close of the sixteenth century, France was invaded by a horde of mountebanks in showy and fantastic garb, who went from one town to another, loudly and with brazen effrontery proclaiming in the market-places their ability to cure every kind of ailment. And the people, then as now easily duped, lent willing ears to these wily pretenders, and bought freely of their marvellous pills and pellets.[219:1]

The prevalence of quackery in England is shown by a preamble to a statute of Henry VIII, as follows: "Forasmuch as the science and cunning of Physic and Surgery are daily, within this Realm, exercised by a great number of ignorant persons, of whom the greater part have no insight in the same, nor in any other kind of learning. Some also ken no letters on the book; so far forth that common artificers, as smiths, weavers and women, boldly and accustomably take upon them great cures, in which they partly use scorcery and witchcraft, and partly apply such remedies to the disease as being very noxious and nothing meet; to the high displeasure of God, great infamy to the Faculty, and the grievous damage and destruction of divers of the King's people, most especially of them that cannot discern the cunning from the uncunning."

Probably Dr. Gilbert Skeene, of Aberdeen, Scotland, had in mind such pretenders, when he wrote, in a treatise on the Plague, published in 1568, that "Medicineirs[219:2] are mair studious of their ain helthe nor of the common weilthe."

A statute of the thirty-fourth year of Henry VIII (1543) contains the statement that although the majority of the members of the craft of chirurgeons had small cunning, yet they would accept large sums of money, and do little therefor; by reason whereof their patients suffered from neglect.

At about this period, many were the marvellous remedies which were advertised, and keen was the rivalry among empirics, in their efforts to outdo their brethren in the selection of high-sounding names for their vaunted panaceas. Among the latter were to be found such choice nostrums as rectifiers of the vitals, which were warranted to supply the places of all other medicines whatsoever.

Other pleasing remedies rejoiced in the names of vivifying drops, cephalic tinctures, gripe-waters, and angelical specifics.

"The Anatomyes of the True Physition and Counterfeit Mounte-banke" (imprinted at London, 1605) contains an enumeration of some of the classes of people wherefrom recruits were drawn to swell the ranks of charlatans in England some three centuries ago. Such were:

Runagate Jews, the cut-throats and robbers of Christians, slow-bellied monks, who have made escape from their cloisters, simoniacal and perjured shavelings, busy Sir John lack-Latins, thrasonical and unlettered chemists, shifting and outcast pettifoggers, light-headed and trivial druggers and apothecaries, sun-shunning night-birds and corner-creepers, dull-pated and base mechanics, stage-players, jugglers, peddlers, prittle-prattling barbers, filthy graziers, curious bath-keepers, common shifters and cogging cavaliers, bragging soldiers, lazy clowns, one-eyed or lamed fencers, toothless and tattling old wives, chattering char-women and nurse-keepers, long-tongued midwives, 'scape-Tyburns, dog-leeches, and such-like baggage. In the next rank, to second this goodly troupe, follow poisoners, enchanters, wizards, fortune-tellers, magicians, witches and hags. Now, if you take a good view of these sweet companions, you shall find them, not only dolts, idiots and buzzards; but likewise contemners and haters of all good learning.

For the greater part of them disdain book-learning, and never came where learning grew. . . . They are such as cannot abide to take any pains or travel in study. They reject incomparable Galen's learned Commentaries, as tedious and frivolous discourses, having found through Paracelsus's Vulcanian shop, a more short way to the Wood. . . . Others are so notoriously sottish, that being over head and ears in the myrie puddle of gross ignorance, yet they will by no means see or acknowledge it.

For to give an instance in the most absolute, exquisite and divine frame of man's body, if they can shew a rude description thereof, hanging in their chamber, and nickname two or three parts, (so as it would make a horse to break his halter to hear them) they think themselves jolly fellows, and are esteemed great anatomists in the eyes of the Vulgar. . . .

Now it is the honestest and safest course for good and learned physicians, to have no society with these barbarians, enemies to all antiquity, humanity and good learning, lest they hear the old saying, like will to like. As was said of the Devil dancing with the collier.[222:1]

We may glean some information about the methods of the practising quacks of the seventeenth century, from the following announcement, which is to be found in Cotgrave's "Treasury of Wit and Language" (1665):

"My name is Pulsefeel, a poor Doctor of Physick, That does wear three-pile velvet in his hat, Has paid a quarter's rent of his house beforehand, And (simple as he stands here) was made doctor beyond sea. I vow, as I am right worshipful, the taking Of my degree cost me twelve French crowns, and Thirty-five pounds of butter in Upper Germany. I can make your beauty and preserve it, Rectifie your bodie and maintaine it, Clarifie your blood, surfle your cheeks, perfume Your skin, tinct your hair, enliven your eye, Heighten your appetite; and as for Jellies, Dentifrizes, Dyets, Minerals, Fricasses, Pomatums, Fumes, Italia masks to sleep in, Either to moisten or dry the superficies, Faugh! Galen Was a goose and Paracelsus a Patch, to Doctor Pulsefeel."

FOOTNOTES:

[202:1] There is a legend of a certain physician, who would never eat roast duck, because certain members of that impolite bird's tribe had addressed insulting remarks to him.

[202:2] Book ii, x, 2.

[203:1] An Enquiry into Dr. Ward's Practice of Physick; London, Printed for J. Humphrey at the Pamphlet Shop, next to the Artichoke, near Great Turn-Stile in Holburn, 1749.

[203:2] Second Series, vol. iii; 1857.

[206:1] The New World, vol. ii; 1893.

[206:2] Dr. Hugo Magnus, Superstition in Medicine.

[208:1] Universal Cyclopedia and Atlas, 1908.

[210:1] Dr. Hugo Magnus, Superstition in Medicine.

[210:2] The International Monthly, vol. v; 1902.

[210:3] Vol. ii.

[211:1] Montreal Medical Journal, vol. xxxi; 1902.

[212:1] Edward Berdoe, The Origin and Growth of the Healing Art.

[213:1] Charaka, Samhita, vol. iii, p. 8.

[214:1] Vol. ii, p. 108.

[215:1] Social England, vol. ii, p. 104.

[216:1] Practitioner, vol. lxviii; 1902.

[218:1] M. D. Synge, A Short History of Social Life in England.

[218:2] Dr. Theodor Puschmann, A History of Medical Education.

[219:1] Larousse, Grand Dictionnaire Universel, art. "Charlatan."

[219:2] This word appears to have been used in the sense of Medicaster, a diminutive of the Latin Medicus, a physician.

[222:1] The spelling of this extract has been modernized.

CHAPTER XIX

QUACKS AND QUACKERY (CONTINUED)

An English physician, who practised during the early part of the reign of King James I, described the charlatan of that period as shameless, a mortal hater of all good men, an adept in cozening, legerdemain, conycatching,[223:1] and all other shifts and sleights; a cracking boaster, proud, insolent, a secret back-biter, a contentious wrangler, a common jester and liar, a runagate wanderer, a cogging[223:2] sychophant and covetous exactor, a wringer of his patients. In a word, a man, or rather monster, made of a mixture of all vices.[223:3]

Robert Burton, in "The Anatomy of Melancholy," published in 1621, said that "if we seek a physician as we ought, we may be eased of our infirmities; such a one, I mean, as is sufficient and worthily so called. For there be many mountebanks, quack-salvers and empiricks, in every street almost, and in every village, that take upon them this name, and make this noble and profitable art to be evil spoken of and contemned by reason of these base and illiterate artificers. . . . Many of them to get a fee, will give physick to every one that comes, without cause."

That original genius, Daniel Defoe (1661-1731), in his "Description of a Quack Doctor," wrote that sometimes he would employ the most vulgar phrases imaginable, and again he would soar out of sight and traverse the spacious realms of fustian and bombast. He was, indeed, very sparing of his Latin and Greek, as (God knows) his stock of those commodities was but slender. But then, for hard words and terms, which neither he, nor you, nor I, nor anybody else could understand, he poured them out in such abundance that you'd have sworn he had been rehearsing some of the occult philosophy of Agrippa, or reading extracts from the Cabala.

"If a man doth but write a book," observed an old author, "or at least transcribe a great part of it, word for word, out of another book, and give it a new title, he is naturally regarded by the ignobile vulgus as a famous doctor, especially if he write M.D. after his name. But let none of these poor shifts or sleights deceive you. You will quickly see that the drift of such publication was only to sell off some Packets of Quack Remedies, and hedge you into his clutches, where 'tis odds but he will pinch, if he does not gripe you to death."[225:1]

In the old Province of Languedoc, in Southern France, charlatans were liable to be summarily dealt with. For when any mountebank appeared in the city of Montpellier, the magistrates were empowered to set him astride of a meagre, miserable ass, with his face to the animal's tail.

Thus placed, the wretched mountebank was made to traverse the streets of the town, his progress meanwhile being enlivened by the hooting and shouts of the children, and the ironical jeers of the populace.[225:2]

The facility wherewith ignorant persons may acquire a reputation for skill in Medicine, is exemplified by the following anecdote. A Staffordshire cobbler had somehow gotten possession of a parcel of medical receipts, and made such diligent use thereof, that he not only was speedily invested with the title of Doctor, but likewise became famous in the neighborhood on account of some alleged remarkable cures. Thereupon he laid aside his awl to assume the dignity of a charlatan. It happened that a young lady of fortune fell ill about that time, and her mother was induced to send for the newly fledged Esculapian. The latter, after examining the patient, remarked that he would go home and consider the case, as he never prescribed rashly. Accordingly in looking over his recipes, he found one which tickled his fancy, although the directions, "to be taken in a proper vehicle," mystified him. Nothing daunted, he consulted a dictionary and found that a vehicle was either a coach, cart or wheel-barrow. Highly elated, he hastened to inform the young lady's mother that her coach must be gotten ready at once, and that her daughter must get into it and take the remedy which he had brought. But the lady would not consent, alleging the risk of exposure to the outside air. "Well," said the rascally quack, "you must then order a wheel-barrow to be sent to your daughter's room, for this medicine must be taken in a proper vehicle, and in my opinion a wheel-barrow will answer the purpose as well as a coach."[226:1] Can any one doubt that the wheel-barrow furnished a powerful therapeutic suggestion in this case?

In the early part of the eighteenth century, it appears that charlatans were very numerous in England. Indeed the "corps of medical savages" was almost as motley and manifold in form as in the Middle Ages. The dabblers in medicine included grocers, book-sellers, printers, confectioners, merchants and traders, midwives, medical students, preachers, chemists, distillers, gipsies, shepherds, conjurors, old women, sieve-makers and water-peddlers. Apothecaries were permitted to sell drugs to "alchemists, bath-servants and ignorant quacks, while dabsters, calf-doctors, rag-pickers, magicians, witches, crystallomancers, sooth-sayers and other mancipia [purchased slaves] of the Devil, were allowed to practice Medicine."[227:1]

At this same period, we are told, the mass of the English people were extraordinarily credulous. And this fact was true, not only of the densely ignorant class, but also of the more intelligent and better educated middle class, who were ready to believe everything that appeared in print.[227:2] Hence was afforded an ideal field for the exercise of the wily charlatan's activities. And the glowing advertisements of quack remedies appealed strongly to the popular fancy.

A London surgeon, Dr. P. Coltheart, writing in 1727, asserted that English practitioners of that time were the peers of any in Europe. He complained, however, of the multitude of ignorant quacks, who were allowed a free hand in the practice of their pretended art, to the detriment of the community.

The spectacle of such a gallant array of charlatans, recruited from the ranks of illiterate tramps and vagrants, the very scum of society, yet thriving by reason of the popular credulity, certainly warranted the scathing arraignment of these interlopers by reputable physicians, who thus found a vent for their righteous indignation, although they were powerless to impede thereby the strong tide of imposture.

How often it happened, wrote William Connor Sydney, in "England and the English in the Eighteenth Century," that a bricklayer (who chanced to be the seventh son of his father), or a sharp-witted cobbler, picked up an antiquated collection of medieval recipes, and perused it in his leisure hours! Then, dispensing with his trowel or awl, he devoted himself to the sale of pellets, lotions and gargles, possessing marvellous virtues!

Here is a copy of an advertisement which appeared in an early number of the London "Spectator":

Loss of Memory or Forgetfulness certainly cured by a grateful electuary, peculiarly adapted for that end. It strikes at the primary source, which few apprehend, of Forgetfulness, makes the head clear and easy, the spirits free, active and undisturbed; corroborates and revives all the noble faculties of the soul, such as thought, judgment, apprehensions, reason and memory, which last in particular it so strengthens as to render that faculty exceeding quick and good beyond imagination, thereby enabling those whose memory was almost totally lost, to remember the minutest circumstances of their affairs, etc; to a wonder. Price 2s. 6d a pot. Sold only at Mr. Payne's, at the Angel and Crown, in St. Paul's Church-Yard, with directions.

William Smith, in his "History of the Province of New York from its First Discovery to the Year 1722" (London, 1757), wrote as follows:

The History of our Diseases belongs to a Profession with which I am very little acquainted. Few physicians amongst us are eminent for their skill. Quacks abound like Locusts in Egypt, and too many have recommended themselves to a full Practice and profitable subsistence. This is the less to be wondered at, as the Profession is under no Kind of Regulation. Loud as the call is, to our Shame be it remembered, we have no Law to protect the Lives of the King's Subjects from the Malpractice of Pretenders. Any man at his Pleasure sets up for Physician, Apothecary and Chirurgeon. No candidates are either examined or licensed, or even sworn to fair practice. In 1753 the City of New York alone boasted the Honour of having forty Gentlemen of that Faculty.

A contributor to the Cincinnati "Lancet and Observer," October, 1861, moralized on this subject in a somewhat pessimistic vein.

To see an ignorant, boastful quack petted, caressed and patronized by people of culture and refinement, wrote he, such as members of the learned professions, statesmen, philosophers, shrewd merchants and bankers, as well as by worthy mechanics and trusting farmers, is enough to make one ponder whether after all it is worth while to devote money, time and talents in acquiring a thorough knowledge of professional duties. . . . However natural such a method of reasoning, it will not influence the sober mens conscia recti of the trained physician.

In an address before the Medical and Surgical Society of Baltimore, January

17, 1859, Dr. Lewis H. Steiner defined quackery as that mode of practising medicine, which adopts one and the same remedy for every disease, of whatever origin or nature. Quackery, wherever found, is based upon a misapplication of some recognized principle or fact, and hence invariably presupposes the existence of a modicum of truth, as its starting-point.

Precisely as the counterfeit coin has a certain value with the unwary, on account of its resemblance to that which is genuine, so all quackery must proceed from a false application of a known truth, or an attempted imitation of this truth in various forms.

An analogy was drawn between a quack and the weaker animal in a dog-fight by a writer in "The Boston Medical and Surgical Journal," April 1, 1846. For, said he, it is a trait of human nature to side with the under-dog. And it is this trait which causes some people to be pleased at the quack's success, for they regard him, in a sporting sense, as a little dog, and demand for him fair play. The maudlin sympathies of such persons are aroused by the sight of an adventurer striving against odds, with one sole end in view, namely, the accumulation of shekels under false pretences.

Probably at no period in the world's history has charlatanry been more flourishing than during the first decade of the twentieth century, and that too in the face of unexampled progress in medical Science. The reason is not far to seek. The modern quack utilizes the power of the unconscious or subjective mind over the body. This is the effective agency, not only in so-called mental healing, but also in semi-scientific cures of various sorts, in faith-cures, as well as in the cures ascribed to relics and charms.[231:1] The widespread heralding of patent medicines is also founded upon the principle of auto-suggestion. The descriptions of symptoms and diseases in the advertisements of charlatans, suggest morbid ideas to the objective mind of the reader. These ideas, being then transferred to his subjective mind, exert an unwholesome influence upon his bodily functions.[231:2] His next procedure is the trial of some vaunted nostrum. Thus the shrewd empiric thrives at the expense of his fellow men. He takes a mean advantage of their credulity, though probably in most cases unaware of the vicious psychological processes, which render many his willing dupes.

It has been aptly remarked that the public is ever more ready to believe pleasing fictions, than disagreeable verities. Populus vult decipi, trite saying though it be, is as true to-day as at any time in the past. If it were not so, quackery could not thrive. Gladly the people "honors pay to those who on their understandings most impose." Apropos of the methods of charlatans, is the story of a certain Scotch farmer, whose success in selling his cattle at high prices aroused the curiosity of his neighbors. One day, when fuddled with drink, after much coaxing, he revealed the secret by saying: "On going to sell my beasties, I first finds a fool, and then I shoves 'em on to him."[232:1]

Dr. William Osler, in his "Aequanimitas and Other Addresses" (1904), remarked that "Knowledge comes, but wisdom lingers"; and in matters medical the ordinary citizen of to-day has not one whit more sense than the Romans of old, whom the witty Greek writer Lucian scourged for a credulity which made them fall easy victims to the quacks of the second century. Man has an inborn craving for medicine. Heroic dosing for several generations has given his tissues a thirst for drugs; and now that the pharmacists have cloaked even the most nauseous remedies, the temptation is to use physic on every occasion.

Dudley F. Sicher, in the "Popular Science Monthly," September, 1905, comments on the enormous development of quackery, which has been more than commensurate with the growth of medical science and the advance of western civilization, in recent years. According to this authority, the number of resident quacks in Berlin, Germany, has increased sixteen-fold since 1874. And in New York City, there are approximately twenty thousand, against six thousand regular practitioners. "Given on the one hand the limitations of scientific medicine, the dread of disease, and the power of auto-suggestion, and on the other hand, depraved humanity, hard-driven in the struggle for existence, and you have the essential parts, which, with a few minor pieces, make up the quackery machine. . . . Psycho-therapeutics and knowledge of human nature make up the quack's entire outfit." The popular distrust of legitimate Medicine facilitates a recourse to the alleged marvellous specifics and panaceas, so extensively advertised; lineal descendants of the magical remedies of old.

Then, too, the secrecy and mystery associated with the remedies of quacks, appeal strongly to the popular fancy.

Charles Dickens wrote in "Barnaby Rudge" that it was only necessary to invest anything, however absurd, with an air of mystery, in order to give it a secret charm and power of attraction, which people are unable to resist. False prophets, he said, false priests, false doctors, false prodigies of whatever kind, veiling their proceedings in mystery, have always addressed themselves at an immense advantage, to the popular credulity, and have been, perhaps, more indebted to that resource in gaining and keeping for a time the upper hand of Truth and Common Sense, than to any half-dozen items in the whole catalogue of imposture. To awaken curiosity and to gratify it by slow degrees, yet leaving something always in suspense, is to establish the surest hold that can be had, in wrong, on the unthinking portion of mankind.

Unscrupulous charlatans have shrewdness enough to make free use of the power of suggestion in their nefarious practice, though oftentimes doubtless wholly ignorant of its mode of action. The great majority of them, while probably unaware of the existence of subconscious mental life, have always had a vivid realization of the positive fact of the gullibility of human nature, a fact which affords them the keenest pleasure and enduring satisfaction.

One can well imagine that the winning smile which often illumines the features of a sleek and crafty pretender, is supplanted by audible chuckling when he retires from company. Having long since gotten rid of his conscience, he can afford to be merry at the expense of his fellow creatures.

It has been aptly said that no amount of instruction in physiology or materia medica at medical colleges will have any influence in the suppression of quackery. But the recognition and utilization, by the profession, of the wonderful forces of psycho-therapy will have such an influence, because light will thereby be shed upon the methods of the charlatan, whose operations will then no longer be shrouded from the public view in mystery, wherein has lain for many centuries their most potent charm.

The author of "Physic and Physicians" (London, 1839) remarks that a doctor should always have ready an answer to every question which a lady may put to him, for the chances are that she will be satisfied with it. Moreover he should invariably diagnose an affection with celerity; and rather than betray ignorance of the seat of a disorder, it were better, says this writer, to assign it at once to the pancreas or pineal gland. A lady once asked her apothecary, an ignorant fellow, regarding the composition of castor oil, and seemed quite content with his reply, that it was extracted from the beaver. Another patient asked her physician how long she was likely to be ill, and was told that it depended largely on the duration of the disease. A certain doctor, probably a quack, acquired some notoriety by always prescribing the left leg of a boiled fowl. Reiteration of the superior nutritive qualities of that member, and positive assertions of the comparative worthlessness of the right leg, doubtless impressed the patients' minds in a salutary manner.

A writer in "Putnam's Magazine," August, 1909, commends the so-called Emmanuel Movement as capable of benefiting many, in all stations of life. He says further that the wicked and the charlatan may enter upon the practice of psycho-therapy, but in a majority of cases, the sub-conscious mind, upon which the healer works, will reject the evil suggestion of the practitioner who strives to use his powers for malign purposes. That is the almost unanimous verdict of the psychological experts. If the old proverb be true, "In vino veritas," so in the hypnotic state the real bent of the normal mind and personality is more ready to follow the good and reject the bad suggestion, than in the normal, conscious state. Instinctive morality comes to the aid of the genuine psycho-therapist, and refuses its cooperation to the counterfeit.

In the United States, the door yawns wider for the admission of charlatans than in any other country. The demand for panaceas and for the services of those who pretend to cure by unusual methods, is not limited to persons who are wanting in intelligence, or to those who are weakened and discouraged by exhausting diseases. So long as the love of the marvellous exists, there will be a certain demand for quackery, and the supply will not be wanting.[236:1]

Probably in no region of the world does there exist a more attractive field for medical pretenders, than the thickly settled foreign settlements of the city of New York. Here they may thrive and fatten, as they ply their nefarious trade, doubtless slyly laughing the while, on account of the simplicity of their helpless victims. The poor hungry wretch who steals a loaf of bread is held legally accountable for the theft, and if caught, he is punished therefor. The unscrupulous quack, by reason of his shrewdness, goes scot-free, though a vastly greater villain. To quote from a recent editorial in the "New York Times": "A course in medicine and surgery is expensive, and takes a lot of time, while a varied assortment of pseudo-religious and pseudo-philosophic phrases can be learned in a few days by any man or woman with a disinclination for honest work."

A recent English writer argued that it were folly to attempt the suppression of quackery by statute; for, says he, the freeborn Anglo-Saxon considers that he has the inalienable right of going to the Devil in his own way. And he resents anything like dictation in the sphere of medicine, as much as in religion.

FOOTNOTES:

[223:1] Thieves' slang for cheating.

[223:2] One who used loaded dice in gambling.

[223:3] Beware of Pick-Purses, or a Caveat for Sick Folkes to take heede of unlearned Physitions and unskilfull Chyrurgians. By F. H., Doctor in Physick. Imprinted at London, 1605.

[225:1] The Modern Quack or Medicinal Impostor. London. Printed for Thomas Warner, at the Black Boy, in Pater Noster Row, 1724.

[225:2] Cautions and Advice to the Public respecting some Abuses in Medicine, through the Malpractices of Quacks or Pretenders, by William Jackson. London. [No date.]

[226:1] P. Coltheart, Surgeon, London, 1727.

[227:1] Joh. Hermann Baas, History of Medicine, p. 771.

[227:2] Social England, vol. v. p. 66.

[231:1] A. T. Schofield, M.D., The Unconscious Mind, pp. 334-5.

[231:2] Dr. John Duncan Quackenbos, Hypnotic Therapeutics, p. 88.

[232:1] John D. Jackson, M.D., The Black Arts in Medicine.

ADDENDA

COPY OF CERTIFICATE

These may Inform all whom it might Concern, that Mr. John Kaighin, of the Province of West New Jersey, hath lived with me (here under named) a considerable time, as a Disciple, to learn the Arts and Mysteries of Chymistry, Physick, and the Astral Sciences, whereby to make a more Perfect Discovery of the Hidden Causes of more Occult and Uncommon Diseases, not so easily to be discovered by the Vulgar Practice. In all which he has been very Dilligent and Studious, as well as in the Administration of the Medecines, and in the various Cases: wherein his Judgment may be safely depended upon in all things, so far as he follows my Instructions. And Hope he may in all things answer the Confidence that may be reposed in him. C. WITT. GERMANTOWN, Febr. 20, 1758.

Following is a Prayer for a Dyspeptic, drawn up by an adherent of Christian Science:

Holy Reality, Blessed Reality, believing that Thou art everywhere present, we believe that Thou art in this patient's stomach, in every fibre, in every cell, in every atom; that Thou art the sole, only Reality of that stomach. Heavenly, Holy Reality, Thou art not sick, and therefore nothing in this universe was ever sick, is now sick, or can be sick. We know, Father and Mother of us all, that there is no such thing as a really diseased stomach; that the disease is the Carnal Mortal Mind given over to the World, the Flesh and the Devil; that the mortal mind is a twist, a distortion, a false attitude, the Hamartia [+hamartia+, sin] of Thought.

Help us to stoutly affirm, with our hand in your hand, with our eyes fixed on Thee, that we never had Dyspepsia, that we will never have Dyspepsia, that there is no such thing, that there never was any such thing, that there never will be any such thing. Amen.[239:1]

FOOTNOTES:

[239:1] The Faith and Works of Christian Science.

APPENDIX

SOME NOTED IRREGULAR PRACTITIONERS

PARACELSUS

THEOPHRASTUS BOMBASTUS VON HOHENHEIM, commonly known as Paracelsus, was born in 1493 at Maria Einsiedeln, near Zurich, Switzerland. When he was nine years old, his father, who was a reputable physician, removed his residence to Carinthia. Paracelsus received instruction in chemistry from the Abbot Trithemius, a Benedictine monk, and then investigated mining methods, and learned the physical properties of minerals, ores, and metals. He also studied at universities in France, Germany, and Italy. Quite early in his career he developed a taste for a Bohemian mode of life and is reported to have gained a livelihood by psalm-singing, astrological prescriptions, chiromancy, and even by the practice of the Black Art. He was also keen in acquiring information about popular remedies and nostrums, from travelling mountebanks, barbers, old women, and pretenders of all kinds. In 1526 he was appointed Professor of the Theory and Practice of Medicine at the University in Basle. Here he taught doctrines of his own, denouncing the prevailing tenets of Medical Science, as derived from the ancients, and claiming for himself a supremacy over all other teachers and writers. According to his view, Philosophy, Astrology, Alchemy and Virtue were the four pillars of Medicine. It is a problem how to reconcile his ignorance, his weakness and superstition, his crude notions and erroneous observations, his ridiculous inferences and theories, with his grasp of method, his lofty views of the true scope of Medicine, his lucid statements, his incisive and epigrammatic criticisms of men and motives.[244:1] After remaining at Basle for about a year, he resumed his wanderings, frequenting taverns and spending whole nights in carousals, with the lowest company. Paracelsus believed that it was reserved for him to indicate the right path to the medical practitioners of his day. In carrying out this idea, he exhibited such colossal conceit, and indulged in such virulent abuse of his medical brethren, that he became the object of their hatred and persecution.[244:2]

According to his doctrine, man is a little world or microcosm, and in him are represented all the elements which are to be found in the great world or macrocosm. Some diseases, he averred, require earthy remedies, others aqueous or atmospheric, and still others, igneous. Paracelsus was thoroughly imbued with the cabalistic theories prevalent in his time, and traced analogies between the stars and various portions of the human body. His fame as the greatest of charlatans appears to have been due in large measure to his influence over the popular imagination by the magic power of high-sounding words, which were mostly beyond the comprehension of his hearers. His teachings have been aptly described as a system of dogmatic and fantastic pseudo-philosophy. The following quotation may serve as an illustration.

All these recipes which are prepared for elemental diseases, consist of six things, two of which are from the planets, two from the elements, and two from narcotics. For although they can be composed of three things, one out of each being taken, yet these are too weak for healing purposes. Now there are two which derive from the planets, because they conciliate and correct medicine; two derive from the elements, in order that the grade of the disease may be overcome. Lastly, two are from the narcotics, because the four parts already mentioned are too weak of themselves to expel a disease before the crisis. Observe then, concerning composition, to forestall the critical day. Recipes prepared in this manner, are very helpful for diseases in all degrees of acuteness.

Paracelsus was the first to promulgate the theory of the existence of magnetic properties in the human body, maintaining that the latter was endowed with a double magnetism, of which one portion attracted to itself the planets, and was nourished by them; whence came wisdom, thought, and the senses. The other portion attracted to itself the elements; whence came flesh and blood. He also asserted that the attractive and hidden virtue of man resembles that of amber and of the magnet, and that this virtue may be employed by healthy persons for the cure of disease in others. Thus probably originated the idea which developed into Animal Magnetism, and from it Anton Mesmer is said to have derived inspiration some two hundred years later. Paracelsus died at Salzburg, Austria, in 1541.

In the words of that eminent English divine, Thomas Fuller (1608-1661),

Paracelsus boasted of more than he could do, did more cures seemingly than really, more cures really than lawfully, of more parts than learning, of more fame than parts, a better physician than a man, and a better chirurgeon than physician.

Paracelsus was a very prince among quacks, for probably no man ever talked more loudly and ostentatiously or made vainer pretensions. He was emphatically a knavish practitioner of medicine, a master of the art of puffery, and was phenomenally successful in achieving notoriety. Whatever his natural talent may have been, says Edward Meryon, M.D.,[246:1] he placed himself in the category with those of the same nature, who have ever been ready to purchase this world's riches at the ruinous price of character and reputation.

The system of Paracelsus was founded upon mysticism and fanaticism of the grossest kind. The chief aim of his doctrine was the blending of mysticism and therapeutics, and the creation thereby of a false science, wherewith he sought to exert an influence over the ignorant classes.

According to the cabalistic doctrine, the various events of life and all natural phenomena are due to influences exerted by gods, devils, and the stars. Each member and principal organ of the human body was supposed to correspond with some planet or constellation. Similar foolish ideas were widely prevalent, especially in Germany. Paracelsus was an ignoramus, who affected to despise all the sciences, because of his lack of knowledge of them. While prating much about divine light as the source of all learning and culture, his boorish mien and rude manners afforded evidence that he did not profit much by its happy influence.[246:2]

The Paracelsians maintained that life is a perpetual germinative process, controlled by the archaeus or vital force, which was supposed to preside over all organic phenomena. The principal archaeus was believed to have its residence in the stomach, but subordinates guarded the interests of the other important bodily organs.

Nature was sufficient for the cure of the majority of ills. But when the internal physician, the man himself, was tired or incapable, some remedy had to be applied, which should antagonize the spiritual seed of the disease.[247:1] Such remedies, known as arcana, were alleged to possess marvellous efficiency, but their composition was kept secret. That is to say, they were quack medicines.

Paracelsus maintained that a man who, by abstraction of all sensuous influences, and by child-like submission to the will of God, has made himself a partaker of the heavenly intelligence, becomes thereby possessed of the philosopher's stone. He is never at a loss. All creatures on earth and powers in heaven are submissive to him; he can cure all diseases, and can himself live as long as he chooses, for he holds the elixir of life, which Adam and the early fathers employed before the Flood, and by which they attained to great longevity.

The philosopher's stone, known also as the great elixir, or the red tincture, when shaken in very small quantity into melted silver, lead or other metal, was said to transmute it into gold. In minute doses it was supposed to prolong life and restore youth, and was then called elixir vit?[247:2] Says Ben Jonson in "The Alchemist" (1610), "He that has once the Flower of the Sun, the perfect Ruby which we call Elixir . . . by its virtue can confer honour, love, respect, long life; give safety, valour, yea and victory, to whom he will. In eight and twenty days he'll make an old man of fourscore a child."

Paracelsus was foremost among a group of extraordinary characters, who claimed to be the representatives of science at the close of the Middle Ages. These men were of a bold, inquisitive temper, and with all their faults, they had a noble thirst for knowledge. "Better the wildest guess-work, than that perfect torpor which follows the parrot-like repetition of the words of a predecessor!"[248:1] These irregular practitioners, however impetuous and ill-balanced, were pioneers in opening up new fields of investigation, and in exploring new paths, which facilitated the progress of their successors in the search for scientific truths.

AGRIPPA

HEINRICH CORNELIUS AGRIPPA VON NETTESHEIM, a German alchemist, philosopher, and cabalist, of noble ancestry, was born at Cologne, on the Rhine, September 14, 1486. Having received a liberal education and being by nature versatile, he became in his youth a secretary at the Court of the

German Emperor, Maximilian I.

He served moreover in the army under that monarch, during several Italian campaigns, and by reason of gallantry, won the spurs of a knight. Becoming averse to the profession of arms, he studied with avidity law, medicine, philosophy, and languages, and in 1509 became Professor of Hebrew in the department of Jura, France. Here his caustic humor and intemperate language involved him in quarrels with the monks, while his restless disposition impelled him to rove in search of adventure. He visited successively London, Pavia, and Metz, where he became a magistrate and town orator.

Having expressed opinions contrary to the prevalent beliefs in regard to saints and witches, he was forced to depart abruptly. We next hear of him as a practising physician in Fribourg, Switzerland. Thereafter he became a vagabond and almost a beggar. Like his contemporary, Paracelsus, he advanced the most paradoxical theories during his adventurous career, which latter was partly scientific and partly political, but always turbulent. Finally he established himself at Lyons, where he again practised medicine, and became physician to Louise of Savoy, Regent of France, and the mother of Francis I. Here Agrippa soon fell into disgrace and was banished. In 1528 he joined the Court of Margaret of Austria, ruler of the Netherlands, at Antwerp. On the publication of his work, "On the Vanity of the Sciences," he was imprisoned for a year at Brussels.

Upon his release, he returned to Lyons, where he was again detained in custody, on account of an old libel against his former patroness.

His death occurred at Grenoble, France, February 18, 1535.

Agrippa was possessed of great versatility and learning, but his writings are tinctured with bitterness and satire. He has been described as restless, ambitious, enthusiastic, and credulous, a dupe himself and a deceiver of others. His career was a continuous series of disappointments and quarrels.

Yet he was an earnest searcher after truth, who was fain to attempt the unlocking of Nature's secrets, but did not hold the right key. Profoundly superstitious, he taught, for example, that the herb, Verbena officinalis, vervain, would cure tertian or quartan fevers according to the manner in which it was divided or cut. Agrippa has been tersely described as a "meteor of philosophy."

CARDAN

JEROME CARDAN, an Italian physician, author, mathematician and philosopher, was born at Pavia, September 24, 1501. He was the illegitimate son of Facio Cardan, a man of repute among the learned in his neighborhood, from whom Jerome received instruction in his youth. Although idolized by his mother, he incurred his father's dislike, and these circumstances, we are told, exerted a peculiar influence upon his character. Despite many difficulties, however, he achieved both fame and notoriety. After having received degrees in arts and medicine from the University of Padua, he became Professor of Mathematics at Milan in 1534, and later was admitted to the College of Physicians in that city. In 1547 he declined an invitation to become court physician at Copenhagen, on account of the harsh northern climate and the obligation to change his religion. In the year 1552 Jerome Cardan visited Scotland at the request of John Hamilton, Archbishop of St. Andrews, whom he treated for asthma with success. Thence he was summoned to England to give his professional advice in the case of Edward VI, after which he returned to Milan with enhanced prestige. He afterwards practised Medicine at Pavia and Bologna and finally settled at Rome, where he received a pension from the Pope. His death occurred there, September 21, 1575.

Cardan was possessed of great natural ability, and for a time was regarded as the most eminent physician and astrologer among his contemporaries. But his mind was of a peculiar cast, and his temper most inconstant. He had, says Peter Bayle, in his "Historical Dictionary," a decided love of paradox, and of the marvellous, an infantine credulity, a superstition scarce conceivable, an insupportable vanity, and a boasting that knew no limits. His works, though full of puerilities and contradictions, of absurd tales and charlatanry of every description, nevertheless offer proofs of a bold, inventive genius, which seeks for new paths of science, and succeeds in finding them. According to his own statement, he found pleasure in roaming about the streets all night long. His love of gaming amounted to a mania. Baron von Leibnitz (1646-1716) wrote of Cardan, that notwithstanding his faults, he was a great man, and without his defects, would have been incomparable. He wrote extensively on philosophy, mathematics, and medicine, and also on chiromancy. For his own follies and misfortunes he apologized, attributing them all to the influence of the stars. He has been described as a genuine philosopher and devotee of science, and his lasting reputation is chiefly due to his discoveries in algebra, in which art, wrote the historian, Henry Hallam, he made a great epoch.

BALSAMO

One of the most notorious charlatans of the eighteenth century was Giuseppe Balsamo, who was born at Palermo, Sicily, June 2, 1743. Though of humble origin, this arch-impostor assumed the title of Count Alessandro di Cagliostro, and styled himself Grand Cophta, Prophet and Thaumaturge. He married Lorenza Feliciani, the daughter of a girdle-maker of Rome. Balsamo professed alchemy and free-masonry, practised medicine and sorcery, and raised money by various methods of imposture. He rode about in his own coach, attended by a numerous retinue in rich liveries. His attire consisted of an iron-gray coat, a scarlet waistcoat trimmed with gold lace, and red breeches. His jaunty hat was adorned with a white feather, and handsome rings encircled his fingers. He carried a sword after the fashion of the times, and his shoe-buckles shone like flashing jewels.

Balsamo was a man of great energy; gifted with persuasive eloquence which seemed to exercise a charm over his hearers. Having rare natural abilities, he enriched his mind by diligent studies and observations of human nature, during his tours abroad. But in spite of these advantages he failed to rise above the sphere of an unscrupulous charlatan.

In 1780 he settled in Strasburg, where he established a reputation by some marvellous cures. Here was the culmination of his fame and fortune. Five years later he came to Paris, where he became implicated in the notorious affair of the "Diamond Necklace," and was imprisoned in the Bastille for some months. His death occurred at the fortress of Saint L 閗 n, Rome, in 1795. A sublimer rascal never breathed, wrote W. Russell, LL.D., in "Eccentric Personages." Balsamo had unlimited faith in the gullibility of mankind, and was amply endowed with the gifts which enable their possessor to shear the simpletons of society.

GREATRAKES

VALENTINE GREATRAKES was born at Affane, County of Waterford, Ireland, on Saint Valentine's Day, February 14, 1628. He was educated a Protestant at the free school of Lismore near his home, and at Trinity College, Dublin.

At the outbreak of the Civil War in 1641, his mother fled with him to England and took refuge in Devonshire, where he devoted himself to the study of the classics and divinity. Afterwards Greatrakes served for seven years in Cromwell's army, holding a commission as lieutenant of cavalry under Roger Boyle, Earl of Orrery. In 1656 he left the army and returned to Affane, where he was appointed a magistrate and served as such with credit.

Soon after the Restoration, in obedience to a divine impulse, he began practice as a healer of various diseases by the method known as laying-on of hands, stroking, or touching, which had been employed by the sovereigns of England, from the time of Edward the Confessor. Greatrakes's success was immediate and phenomenal. People flocked to him so rapidly, we are told, from all quarters, that "his barns and out-houses were crammed with innumerable specimens of suffering humanity." In 1665 he returned to England, where he performed many seemingly marvellous cures; and came to be regarded as a greater miracle-worker than King Charles II himself. But after an investigation and adverse report by members of the Royal Society, his practice fell into disrepute, and he retired to his native land, where he sojourned in obscurity until his death, which is supposed to have occurred after the year 1682. One David Lloyd, a biographer, issued a tract entitled "Wonders no Miracles, or Mr. Valentine Greatrakes' Gift of Healing Examined," wherein he endeavored to show that the famous "Irish stroaker" was little better than an impostor. In reply to this, Greatrakes published a pamphlet, vindicating his methods, with testimonials from persons of quality and distinction.

Greatrakes has been described as a man of unimpeachable integrity, a highly respectable member of society, and incapable of attempting to deceive by fraud. Notoriety was distasteful to him, and in this respect he was above the plane of an ordinary charlatan. An enthusiast, he believed himself to be invested with divine healing powers. His success was surely due to forcible therapeutic suggestions communicated by him to the minds of highly imaginative and credulous people, who reposed confidence in his methods. It mattered not that they believed the cures of their nervous disorders to be wrought solely through the physical agency of laying-on of hands, whereby some mysterious healing force, magnetic or otherwise, was communicated to them.

In attempting an explanation of the cures wrought by Greatrakes, Henry Stubbe, a contemporary writer, affirmed that "God had bestowed upon Mr. Greatarick a peculiar temperament, or composed his body of some particular ferments, and the effluvia thereof, sometimes by a light, sometimes by a violent friction, restore the temperament of the debilitated parts, reinvigorate the blood, and dissipate all heterogeneous ferments out of the bodies of the diseased, by the eyes, nose, hands and feet." There is nothing recorded in regard to Greatrakes's methods (says Professor Joseph Jastrow, in "Fact and Fable in Psychology"), which definitely suggests the production of the hypnotic state; but direct suggestion, reinforced by manipulation, obviously had much to do with the cures.

In 1666 the Chamberlain of the Worcester Corporation expended ten pounds, fourteen shillings in an entertainment for "Mr. Greatrix, an Irishman famous for helping and curing many lame and diseased people, only by stroking of their maladies with his hand and therefore sent for to this and many other places."

From a letter written by Greatrakes to the Archbishop of Dublin, it appears that he believed himself to be inspired of God, for the purpose of curing disease. He received lavish hospitality in many homes, when at the height of his popularity, and was regarded as a phenomenal adept in the art of healing by touch.[257:1]

If there exists such a thing as the "gift of healing," Greatrakes appears to have possessed it. Dr. A. T. Schofield believes that in certain rare cases individuals are endowed with the faculty of curing by touch, to which the terms magnetic, psychic, occult, hypnotic, and mesmeric have been applied. This power is resident in the operator, and has nothing to do with suggestion; whereas in so-called faith-healing, the power is resident in the patient, who, by the exercise of faith, puts it into action.

Greatrakes has been described as having an agreeable personality, pleasant manners, a fine figure, gallant bearing, a handsome face, musical voice, and a good stock of animal spirits. Thus equipped, we may not wonder that he was ever welcome in merry company. He had an impulse or strange persuasion of his own mind (says J. Cordy Jeaffreson, in "A Book about Doctors") that he had the gift of curing the King's Evil. A second impulse gave him the power of healing ague, and a third "inspiration of celestial aura imparted to him command, under certain conditions, over all human diseases." Greatrakes adapted his manipulations to the requirements of individual cases. Oftentimes gentle stroking sufficed, but when the evil spirits were especially malignant, he employed energetic massage. Occasionally the demon fled, "like a well-bred dog," at the word of command, but more frequently the victory was not won until the healer had rubbed himself into a red face, and a copious perspiration.

It is narrated that when Greatrakes was practising in London, a rheumatic and gouty patient came to him. "Ah," said the healer, colloquially, "I have seen a good many spirits of this kind in Ireland. They are watery spirits, who bring on cold shivering and excite an overflow of aqueous humor in our poor bodies." Then, addressing the demon, he continued: "Evil spirit, who has quitted thy dwelling in the waters, to come and afflict this miserable body, I command thee to quit thy new abode, and to return to thine ancient habitation."[258:1]

From among a large number of testimonials of cures performed by Greatrakes, a single example may suffice.

MR. SQUIBB'S LETTER TO MR. BOREMAN

SIR,

Whereas you are pleased to enquire after the Cure, by God's means done upon me, by the stroking of my head by Mr. Greatrakes; These are thoroughly to inform you that being violently troubled with an excessive pain of the head, that I had hardly slept six hours in six days and nights, and taken but very little of sustenance in that time; and being but touch'd by him, I immediately found ease, and (thanks be to God) do continue very well; and do further satisfie you, that the rigour of the pain had put me into a high Fever, which immediately ceas'd with my head-ache: and do likewise further inform you that a Servant being touch'd for the same pain, that had continu'd upon him for twelve years last past, he touch'd him in the forehead, and the pain went backward; and that but by his stroking upon the outside of his cloaths, the pain came down to and out of his foot: the party continues still well. These Cures were wrought about 3 weeks before Easter.

And thus much I assure you to be true from him that is Your Friend and Servant EDM. SQUIBB.

COVENT-GARDEN, April 20, 1666. At my Lady Verney's, the place of my residence.

While Greatrakes acquired great celebrity on account of the numerous cures which he performed, he was unable to explain the nature of his healing powers. In a letter to the Hon. Robert Boyle, he expressed the belief that many of the pains which afflict men, are of the nature of evil spirits. "Such pains," wrote he, "cannot endure my hand, nay, not my glove, but flye immediately, though six or eight coats and cloaks be put between the parties' body and my hand, as at York House, the Lady Ranalough's and divers other places, since I came to London."

VAN HELMONT

JOHANN BAPTIST VAN HELMONT, a celebrated Belgian physician, scholar and visionary, of noble family, was born at Brussels in 1577. At an early age he began the study of medicine, and was appointed Professor of Surgery at the University of Louvain. Becoming, however, infected with the delusions of alchemy, and being possessed of an ardent imagination, he inclined naturally to the study of occult science, and was infatuated with the idea of discovering a universal remedy. He was, moreover, a follower of the eminent theologian, Johann Tauler (1290-1361), founder of mystic theology in Germany. Van Helmont has been described as an enthusiastic and fantastic, though upright friend of the truth. He adhered to the theosophic and alchemistic doctrines of a somewhat earlier epoch, and was an admirer of the dogmatic pseudo-philosophy of Paracelsus.

The German writer, Johann Christian Ferdinand Hoefer (1811-1878), said that Van Helmont was much superior to Paracelsus, whom he took as his model. He had the permanent distinction of revealing scientifically the existence of invisible, impalpable substances, namely gases. And he was the first to employ the word gas as the name of all elastic fluids except common air.[260:1] Van Helmont graduated as Doctor of Medicine in 1599, and after several years of study at different European universities, he returned home and married Margaret van Ranst, a noble lady of Brabant. He then settled down on his estate at Vilvoorden, near Brussels, where he remained until his death in 1644.

Johann Hermann Baas, in his "History of Medicine," characterizes him as a fertile genius in the department of chemistry, but denies that he was a great and independent spirit, outrunning his age, or impressing upon it the stamp of his own individuality. Van Helmont, like many another irregular practitioner, achieved fame by some remarkable cures. It was said of him that his patients never languished long under his care, being always killed or cured within two or three days. He was frequently called to attend those who had been given up by other physicians. And to the latters' chagrin, such patients were often unexpectedly restored to health.[261:1]

A lover of the marvellous, and credulous to the point of superstition, Van Helmont became infatuated with erroneous doctrines. His contemporaries, dazzled, it may be, by the brilliancy of his mental powers, regarded him as an erratic genius, but not as a charlatan.

The term spiritual vitalism has been applied to the philosophy of Van Helmont. He maintained that the primary cause of all organization was Archaeus (Gr. +archaios+, primitive), a term said to have been invented by Basil Valentine, the German alchemist (born 1410).

This has been defined as a spirit, or invisible man or animal, of ethereal substance, the counterpart of the visible body, within which it resides, and to which it imparts life, strength, and the power of assimilating food.[261:2] Archaeus was regarded as the creative spirit, which, working upon the raw material of water or fluidity, by means of a ferment promotes the various actions which result in the development and nutrition of the physical organism. As life and all vital action depended upon archaeus, any disturbance of this spirit was regarded as the probable cause of fevers and other morbid conditions.

FLUDD

ROBERT FLUDD, surnamed "the Searcher," an English physician, writer and theosophist, member of a knightly family, first saw the light at Milgate, Kent, in the year 1574. His father, Sir Thomas Fludd, was Treasurer of War under Queen Elizabeth. Robert was a graduate of St. John's College, Oxford.

After taking his degree in 1598, he followed the example of many another man of original mind, athirst for knowledge of the world, and led a roving life for six years, "in order to observe and collect what was curious in nature, mysterious in arts, or profound in science."

Returning to London in 1605, he entered the College of Physicians, and four years later receiving a medical degree, he established himself at his house in Coleman Street, in the metropolis, where he remained until his death in 1637.

Fludd was a voluminous writer, and one of the most famous savants of his time. He was at once physician, chemist, mathematician, and philosopher. But his chief reputation was due to his system of theosophy. Profoundly imbued with mystical lore, he combined in an incomprehensible jumble the doctrines of the Cabalists and Paracelsians. William Enfield, in the "History of Philosophy," remarks of the peculiarity of this philosopher's turn of mind, that there was nothing which ancient or modern times could afford, under the notion of modern wisdom, which he did not gather into his magazine of science. Fludd was reputed to be a man of piety and great learning, and was an adept in the so-called Rosicrucian philosophy. In his view, the whole world was peopled with demons and spirits, and therefore the faithful physician should lay hold of the armor of God, for he has not to struggle against flesh and blood. He published treatises on various subjects which are replete with abstruse and visionary theories. The title of one of these treatises is as follows: "De Supernaturalis, Naturalis, Praeternaturalis, et Contranaturalis Microcosmi Historia, 1619."

The phenomena of magnetism were ascribed by him to the irradiation of angels. Robert Fludd enjoyed the acquaintance and friendship of many scientists at home and abroad, and was without doubt one of the most versatile and erudite of contemporary British scholars.

He devoted much time to scientific experiments and natural philosophy, and constructed a variety of odd mechanisms, including an automatic dragon and a self-playing lyre.[264:1] Moreover, he was a believer in mystical faith-cures, and in the existence of a kind of dualism in therapeutics, whereby sickness and healing were produced by two antagonistic forces.

NOSTRADAMUS

MICHEL DE NOTREDAME, or NOSTRADAMUS, a celebrated French physician and astrologer, of Jewish ancestry, was born at Saint-Remi, a small town in Provence, December 14, 1503. Both of his grandfathers were practitioners of medicine, and his father, Jacques de Notredame, was a notary of Saint-Remi. Michel studied medicine at Avignon and afterwards at the University of Montpellier, where he took his degree.

During the prevalence of an epidemic in the south of France, he acquired distinction by his zealous ministrations to the stricken peasants, and more especially by some remarkable cures attributed to a remedy of his own invention. After the pestilence had subsided, Notredame devoted many years to travel, after which, in the year 1544, he settled at Salon, a little town in the present Department of Bouches-du-Rhue. During a second visitation of the plague, which raged in Provence, he accepted an invitation from the authorities of Lyons and Aix to visit those places. Although his success in treating patients at this time served to enhance his fame as a practitioner, his chief reputation was due to his capacity as an astrologer. He claimed moreover to have the faculty of reading the future, and became the subject of a bitter controversy. For while he gained many adherents abroad, in his own country he was regarded as little better than a charlatan. He became involved in controversies with his professional confreres, who were jealous of his success and doubtless also suspicious of his methods.

It is worthy of note that the most notorious quacks, often men of genius and education, though mentally ill-balanced, and morally of low standards, have been great travellers and shrewd observers of the weak points in human nature. When such an one becomes ambitious to acquire wealth, he is likely to prove a dangerous person in the community. Notredame was regarded as a visionary by some of his contemporaries, while others believed him to have illicit correspondence with the Devil. Among those who were impressed by his pretensions as a soothsayer, was Catherine de' Medici (regent for her son, Charles IX), who invited him to visit the French Court, where he was received as a distinguished guest.

Michel de Notredame published in 1555 his famous work entitled "Centuries," a collection of prophecies, written in quatrains. His death occurred at Salon, July 2, 1566.

We quote as follows from a rare volume, "The True Prophecies of Michel Nostradamus, Physician to Henry II and Charles IX, Kings of France, translated by Theophilus de Garencieres, Doctor in Physick, London, 1672":

He was popularly believed "to have naturally a genius for the knowing of future things, as he himself confesseth in 2 Epistles to King Henry II, and to Caesar, his own son. And besides that genius, the knowledge of astrology did smooth him the way to discover many future events. He had a greater disposition than others to receive those supernatural lights, and as God is pleased to work sweetly in his creatures, and to give some forerunning dispositions to those graces he intendeth to bestow, it seemeth that to that purpose he did choose our author to reveal him so many wonderful secrets. We see every day that God in the distributing of his graces, carrieth Himself towards us according to our humours and natural inclinations. He employeth those that have a generous martial heart, for the defence of His Church, and the destruction of tyrants.

"He leadeth those of a melancholick humour into Colledges and Colisters, and cherisheth tenderly those that are of a meek and mild disposition.

"Even so, seeing that Nostradamus inclined to this kind of knowledge, He gave him in a great measure the grace of it."

LILLY

WILLIAM LILLY, a famous English astrologer of yeoman ancestry, was born at Diseworth, an obscure village in northwestern Leicestershire, May 1, 1602. In his autobiography he described his native place as a "town of great rudeness, wherein it is not remembered that any of the farmers thereof, excepting my grandfather, did ever educate any of their sons to learning." His mother was Alice, daughter of Edward Barham, of Fiskerton Mills in Nottinghamshire.

When eleven years of age, he was placed in the care of one John Brinsley at Ashby-de-la-Zouch, not far from Diseworth. Here he received instruction in the classics. In April, 1620, he went to London to seek his fortune, and obtained employment as foot-boy and general factotum in the family of one Gilbert Wright, of the parish of St. Clement Danes, a man of property, but without education.

Not long after his master's death in 1627, Lilly married the widow, and being then in comfortable circumstances, devoted considerable time to the pursuit of angling, and became fond of listening to Puritan sermons.[268:1] Having abundant leisure, he was enabled to humor the natural bent of his mind, and to begin the study of astrology, which he continued with zeal, devoting special attention to the magical circle and to the invocation of spirits. Keenly alive to the popular credulity, he claimed the possession of supernatural powers as a fortune-teller and soothsayer, largely as a result of the study of the works of noted astrologers, including the "Ars Notoria" of Cornelius Agrippa.

Becoming a prey to melancholy and hypochondria, he lived in retirement for five years at Hersham in Surrey, and then returned to London in 1641. At this time, wrote Lilly in his autobiography, "I took careful notice of every grand action between king and parliament, and did first then incline to believe that, as all sublunary affairs depend on superior causes, so there was a possibility of discovering them by the configuration of the heavens."

In 1644 he published his first almanac, under the title, "Merlinus Angelicus Junior, the English Merlin Revived, or a Mathematical Prediction of the English Commonwealth." This publication was issued annually for nearly forty years, and found a ready sale, being shrewdly adapted to the popular taste. Lilly was said to have acquired considerable influence over the credulous monarch, Charles I, who was wont to consult him regarding political affairs. He was an adept in the wily arts of the charlatan, achieving notoriety by unscrupulous methods. Not a few of his exploits, wrote one of his biographers, indicate rather the quality of a clever police detective, than that of a profound astrologer.

After the Restoration, Lilly fell into disrepute, and again retired to his estate at Hersham, where he began the study of Medicine, receiving a license to practise in the year 1670, when sixty-eight years of age. Thenceforth he combined the professions of physic and astrology. His death occurred June 9, 1681.

Among his publications are the following: "Mr. Lillie's Prediction concerning the many lamentable Fires which have lately happened, with a full account of Fires at Home and Abroad." 1676. "Strange news from the East, or a sober account of the Comet or blazing star that has been seen several Mornings of late." 1677.

GASSNER

JOHANN JOSEPH GASSNER, who was regarded as a thaumaturge by his partisans, and as a charlatan by his opponents, was born at Bratz, a village of the Austrian Tyrol, August 20, 1727. He was educated at Innsbruck and Prague, became a priest, and settled at Coire, the capital of the Swiss canton of Grisons. Here he remained for some fifteen years, ministering acceptably to his parishioners. It appears that he then became impressed with the scriptural accounts of the healing of demoniacs, and devoted himself to the study of the works of famous magicians.

Gradually he acquired a reputation as a healer by means of the methods of laying on of hands, conjuration and prayer. Many of the Tyrolese peasantry flocked to him, as did their Irish brethren to Greatrakes. Gassner treated them all without recompense. He believed that the efficiency of his methods was dependent upon the degree of faith of his patients. Some cases he affected to benefit by drugs, others by touch, and still others by exorcism. He was a pioneer in the employment of suggestion, while summoning to his aid the forces of religious faith, prayer and material remedies.

The Bishop of Constance sent for Gassner, and after a careful examination of his methods and beliefs, became convinced of the purity of his character, and of his good faith. The bishop therefore permitted him to continue his practice at Coire and its neighborhood.

Gassner's reputation as a thaumaturge spread throughout Germany and adjacent countries, and he numbered among his patrons many persons of influence. In 1774, upon invitation of the Bishop of Ratisbon, he removed to Ellwangen, in Westemberg, where he is said to have cured many by the mere word of command, Cesset. He died at Bondorf, in the Diocese of Ratisbon, in the year 1779.

The celebrated Dutch physician, Antoine de Haen, who was a contemporary of Gassner, described the latter as a man of jovial temperament, and a sworn foe to melancholy. He did not take advantage of the popular credulity for his own pecuniary gain, and was therefore morally far above the plane of an ordinary charlatan.

FOOTNOTES:

[244:1] Encyclopedia Britannica, art. "Paracelsus."

[244:2] Edward Theodore Withington, Medical History, p. 225.

[246:1] The History of Medicine.

[246:2] P. V. Renouard, History of Medicine, p. 368.

[247:1] Encyclopedia Britannica, art. "Medicine."

[247:2] Century Dictionary.

[248:1] Blackwood's Edinburgh Magazine, June, 1854.

[257:1] The Gentleman's Magazine, part i; 1856.

[258:1] John Timbs, Doctors and Patients, vol. ii, p. 33.

[260:1] Joseph Thomas, Universal Dictionary of Biography, art. "Van Helmont."

[261:1] Rev. Hugh James Rose, A New General Biographical Dictionary.

[261:2] The Century Dictionary.

[264:1] The New International Encyclopedia.

[268:1] Henry Lee, Dictionary of National Biography.